The Inner Space Traveler

Seven Guiding Principles Of Personal Transformation

D. L. Hoefer

Personal Growth/Spirituality/Psychology

Published by DiscoverTheSelf.com in the United States on January 3rd, 2025.

Cover art: Giorgia Madonno: troughart.com
Cover design and layout: D. L. Hoefer
Illustrations: Camstinio: Fiver.com.
Author photo: Beth Weise
Editing: Teresa Fernandez: Er2Pro.com, Elise Hitchings, and Maria D'Marco @ Reedsy.com, and Laurette Reiff

ISBN: 979-8-9859184-0-3

—*The Inner Space Traveler* is a platform for a **non-logical, non-analytical** (non-Aristotelian [1]) approach to wellness that organically aligns the reader with the same organizing forces that evolved a naked, conscious human. Enjoy the voyage.

---

[1] Korzybski, A. *Science and Sanity: An Introduction to Non-Aristotelian Systems and General Semantics, Institute of General Semantics,*

Reviews

"Profound, deep—reflecting the consciousness of Eckhart Tolle's 'The Power of Now.' It reconnects me to my earlier spiritual self."
Tom Pritchard, LMFT. Founder of the Alcott Center, Los Angeles and Culver City, CA; founder of Westside Mental Health Network, Los Angeles, CA; founder of the Orange County Mediation Center; founder of Villagio Senior Living Center, Walsenburg, Co.

"Hoefer's discussions of consciousness motivated me to reconnect with teachings of The Third Karmapa, Ranjung Dorje, and the more current Khenchen Thrangu Rinpoche."
—Carol O'Dowd, MPA, M.Div., Secretary and past President of the Colorado Association of Psychotherapists.

"I enjoyed [your manuscript] and found wise advice and several practices that I plan to follow."
—Robert Mann, Manship Chair in Journalism for the Manship School of Mass Communication at LSU, Communications Director for Louisiana Governor Kathleen Babineaux Blanco, Press Secretary to the 1990 US Senate reelection campaign of J. Bennett Johnston, and helped elect Senator Mary Landrieu, author/coauthor of numerous books.

Reviews

"This is a brave action you've taken, and I urge you to stand firm with your elemental passions and theory as they offer some unique positions that are supportive of readers and their trending/growing interest in understanding their world and beyond the physical." —Maria D'Marco: author, editor.

"Eye-opening, thought-provoking, insightful, deep, mindful, and enlightening."
—Evelyn Barton, Psychotherapist.

"This book has been a comfort of thinking and musing."
—M. D.

"The most honest, clear explanation of bias and self-sabotage I've ever read."
—Teresa Fernandez, Editor.

"With D.H.'s approach, you actually have a shot at transformation."—Owen Dean.

"I can feel myself changing as I read." —Kim: beta reader.

"This is something I would turn to at different times in my life." —C. Smith.

"Now that I know how to change, I see myself changing at a very high rate." —H Wright.

"David shares deep concepts that are crystal clear in simple language that resonate as true."
—Kirk Drake, Group facilitator.

Your experience is subject to the same laws of physics
that cause clouds to appear in a clear blue sky.

—John Samuel Leiby

Contents

Contents

Contents

A Word Of Gratitude

I wish to acknowledge the individuals who collaborated with me in presenting concepts that are both engaging and accessible: Maria D'Marco, Robert Mann, Tom Pritchard, David Bechtel, Robert Astle, Pamela Matthews, Laura Joan Levine, Laurette Reiff, Owen Dean, Zach Tollen, Jen Hanson, Evelyn Barton, Kirk Drake, Carol O'Dowd, Teresa Fernandez, Elise Hutchings, Hannah Wright, James Hoefer, and Keven Holiday (apologies for any names missed). Thank you!

Acknowledgment

John Samuel Leiby was born into poverty in Pittsburgh, Pennsylvania. With only a high school diploma, he obtained employment with Martin Marietta. He began as a draftsman; then, through evening engineering classes, advanced to the Titan missile project, eventually becoming acting head of R & D. Numerous inventions began as his ideas: screw jacks now operate the flaps of airplanes (saving hundreds of pounds of hydraulics), emergency signalers atop traffic lights, cones that deflect the exhaust in missile silos, viewing a plexiglass replica through a polarized lens reveals the stress points of an airplane design…

It occurred to him that personal experience was subject to the same physical laws that allowed airplanes to fly and jet engines to propel. This vision culminated in four metaphysics classes taught every week in Fort Collins, Denver, Boulder, and Colorado Springs from the mid-1970s through the mid-1990s. He wanted to "raise the consciousness along the Colorado front range." He emphasized awareness of phenomena and how the intangible world is governed by the same physical laws that control the tangible. I count myself fortunate to have attended one or more of these classes each week for seventeen years. John is largely unsung, with no academic credentials or publications. I paraphrase him from time to time; much of the structure and organization of this book derives from him.

Introduction

By Maria D'Marco

I would view this book as being more for seasoned and serious seekers due to the breadth of the concepts and ideologies presented. The circular support creates fertile ground for expanded discussions with self and others. This is a book to be talked about, but more so, to talk about the ideas within. This is not a 'traditional' self-help book. It is not meant to define a troublesome issue, give you a 'list' of practices, and then voila! The reader is 'cured'!

This is much closer to philosophy, an armful of information that leads the reader into a consideration construct that forces them to create their own glue for then massaging it all into a pliable, neutral space where the impossible, like disappearing your depression, can happen.

The positive here is that the book could, and I believe will, be a foundation point from which readers feel compelled to tell others about their experience with the knowledge inside. Once readers understand that this isn't a book about 'controlling' anything or even 'letting go' of things, they will want to share the epiphanies they've experienced from reading this book.

Though I said I felt this was a book for the serious, perhaps even advanced seekers out there, I also feel that this book would be a great read for newer seekers, as it presents many postulates that could (by checking out the bibliography) open up new and deeper realms of thought and consideration.

And though the book points primarily to depression, it offers insights that could be applied to any mental or emotional obstacle.

And finally, the subject of historical trauma is extraordinarily timely — it is literally trending in documentaries and the psychological/neurological worlds. Just yesterday, I watched, by happenstance, a documentary film [on Disney no less] that had a segment on exactly that topic! The entire scene was focused on trauma (such as the Holocaust) and stress triggers and genetic structures being altered over time (generation to generation), and used Romania as an example of extended, extreme catastrophic happenings over 500-600 years, and how they had discovered how Romanians seemed more capable of reacting to sudden catastrophe with unusual calm, people claiming that 'something' came over them and they weren't afraid – like they had already experienced this level of threat and their bodies no longer jacked them up with adrenalin…

And as I watched, I grinned like an idiot, because all I thought of was you and your book! So! What we have here, in this book, is a bona fide 'hot' topic!

March 27th, 2022

About The Author

D. L. Hoefer's journey into metaphysical psychology began

in 1978. It was during his time as a Drug/Alcohol Counselor with the Veterans Administration Hospital that he first observed the cause-and-effect relationships between the physical laws, phenomena, and human experience. This unique perspective was instrumental in resolving his lifelong struggle with depression and has since become a major focus of his practice.

Authors' Note:

When I embraced my depression, I jettisoned to a place beyond the light of any stars. I had always been depressed, but this decision to be with what I saw myself to be was darkness upon darkness—and I saw no end to it. There was nothing—no one to relate to—but myself. I could only watch to see what David (me) does, with the question: Why is David the way he is? Answers came through pain and sadness—more pain than I thought a body could hold—but the answers/awarenesses were exhilarating, so I stayed with the pain—even finding ways to intensify it. I sensed healing: Body/mind, and my hapless identity appeared to be re-orienting. I didn't know the direction these changes would take, but I had to let the truth of them arise. As I share in Chapter 17, "Depression," I awoke one morning after three months of terrible sadness to find my lifelong depression was essentially gone; I felt more connected than ever before.

This occurrence in 1995 has inspired not only this book but also what I've found to be a profound way of relating to life: Instead of choosing a direction, allow yourself to orient to life. Rather than working to "improve" yourself, allow this source that brought you from the elements to self-awareness to evolve *you*. Rather than reading books, identify and learn from the phenomena that surround and incorporate you. Instead of deciding how you want to be, watch as you become—never fully knowing what that is.

Corridors Of Light

D. L. Hoefer

The ways of being are multiplied to infinity
        they fill the spectrum.
They separate out like the great explosion
that began the universe
        and they are all self-reinforcing.
There is no footprint,
        no trodden path.
I am a blind man running through corridors of light
with arms outstretched.
        I am there before the creed.
        I am there before believing.
My truths relate to what I am becoming
        and what I am becoming is forever redefined;
every perception,
every concept,
every attitude,
        changes everything.

Chapter 1

Overview

Very little of the trauma arising out of humanity's horrific history has ever been constructively processed.

Four billion years ago, elements of earth organized into life form. Some think of this organizing force as God. Others think of it as source-energy. I call it consciousness. As life related to the conditions in which it found itself, it became increasingly complex. Out of complexity came the first self-aware thought. It was the first "I am."—Awareness becoming aware of itself.

Feelings and sensations are, I think in large part, the information life used to relate to the conditions in which it found itself. I believe conscious thought evolved from unconscious thought that grew out of feelings and sensations. Because of this, thoughts can trigger feelings, and feelings can trigger thoughts. Thoughts are, therefore, codified feelings.

All the complexity supporting the awareness of *self,* occurred prior to a single self-aware thought. Life organized itself without analysis and without logic into swimming, flying, biting, instinctively reactive creatures based upon the unique conditions in which each entity found itself. For example, fish evading predators crawled onto land and became amphibians. Amphibians, taking advantage of abundant insects and foliage and, no doubt, evading other amphibians, moved inland and, as they adapted, became reptiles.[2] One of these reptiles branched into carnivorous, bipedal theropod dinosaurs like Tyrannosaurus Rex. While many dinosaurs were becoming bigger, meaner, and uglier, a branch of these theropods (Paraves) were becoming smaller, lighter, and cuter: their alligator jaws became beaks (like the embryos of dinosaurs); they grew feathered arms,[3] which possibly provided warmth for brooding, and assisted in running. These theropods climbed trees with hands and feet to avoid predators and jumped/glided from branch to branch, and as their wings evolved (over millions of years),[4] they escaped into the air as warm-blooded birds. [5, 6]

However, as far as humans are concerned, the natural evolution of life, orienting the individual around their unique condition, has become disrupted, biased—even perverted. This is because, with the evolution of self-awareness, thoughts

---

[2]. Scared Cricket. http://www.michellecaldwell.com/linkfiles/scaredcricket/articles/other/evolution.html

[3] Singer, Emily (2015). "How Dinosaurs Shrank and Became Birds" *Quanta Magazine*. https://www.quantamagazine.org/how-birds-evolved-from-dinosaurs-20150602/

[4] Ibid.

[5] "The Origin of Birds." *Understanding Evolution*. https://evolution.berkeley.edu/what-are-evograms/the-origin-of-birds/

[6] "Evolution of Birds." *Libre Texts Biology*. https://bio.libretexts.org/Bookshelves/Introductory_and_General_Biology/Book:_General_Biology_%28Boundless%29/29:_Vertebrates/29.05:_Birds/29.5B:_Evolution_of_Birds

can be used to mitigate unwanted feelings. Rather than feelings orienting the entity as they have for millions of years, they have become inconvenient —sometimes debilitating—nuisances that we have resisted and invented all manner of beliefs, rituals, rationale (See Chapter 3, "Nothing Is Personal"), and even sciences to nullify. Instead of allowing the experience of depression (See Chapter 17, "Depression"), for example, to orient us chemically, neurologically, and interpersonally—we take a pill, thereby truncating the very information conscious thought evolved from; we actually counteract the organic process of awareness (See Chapter 10, "Your Intangible Self"). The effect is that the conditions (trauma) associated with these "unwanted" feelings have been perpetuated and even reinforced. Very little of the trauma arising out of humanity's horrific history has ever been constructively processed.

For example, Gabriel García Márquez talks about indigenous American Indian children wanting to play cowboys and Indians—but nobody wanted to be the Indian.[7] Indian children "not wanting to be the Indian" become adults beset with anxiety, depression, substance abuse, and heart disease…[8] When whole families and ways of life are destroyed, survivors can understandably disassociate. For this and other reasons, like avoidance of guilt and disgrace,

---

[7] University of Minnesota Extension (2020). "Historical Trauma and cultural healing, " https://extension.umn.edu/trauma-and-healing/historical-trauma-and-cultural-healing

[8] Psych Central, Editors (2022) "How Intergenerational Trauma Impacts Families," https://psychcentral.com/lib/how-intergenerational-trauma-impacts-families

historical trauma has been absorbed into the collective unconscious and passed down from parent to child from time immemorial (See Chapter 9, "You Must Become The Impartial Observer Of Yourself").

The effect of inherited trauma is that an individual can experience a lack of identity and low self-esteem regardless of social class. One can experience futility, hopelessness, and depression, which seems inconsistent with an apparently stable, supportive background—as in the following example:

> *The adjusted prevalence of depressive symptoms was higher in the region [Seoul Korea] with a high socioeconomic status (23.1%) than in the region with a lower economic status (16.6%) (p<0.001)." This tendency was less likely among females.*[9] *U.S. Studies find "income and the composite social class measure showed small positive associations with self-esteem.*[10] [11]

---

[9] Sun-Jin Fo, Hyeon Woo Yim, Myeong He Bang, Mi ol Lee, Tae-Youn Jun, Jin-Sook Choi, Myung-Soo Lee, Won-Chul Lee, and Yong-Moon Park (2011). "The Association between Economic Status and Depressive Symptoms: an Individual and Community Level Approach," *Psychiatry Investigation*, Aug 11.
https://www.ncbi.nlm.nih.gov/pmc/articles/PMC3182383/

[10] Kraus, Michael W, Park, Jun W. (2014). "The Undervalued self: social class and self-evaluation," *Frontiers in Psychology, 5(*December 5).
https://www.frontiersin.org/articles/10.3389/fpsyg.2014.01404/full

[11] Gecas, Viktor, Seff, Monica A. (1990). "Social Class and Self-Esteem: Psychological Centrality, Compensation, and the Relative Effects of Work and Home," *Social Psychology Quarterly 53*(2)
https://www.jstor.org/stable/2786677

Individuals with supportive families can become self-destructive and see themselves as the cause of it all. For instance:

> *Caroline's (1999) storyline is about her 12-year-old self who works hard to uphold her cultural commitments and social obligations, especially in being an ambitious American pupil and responsible daughter. ... "I cut myself and was paradoxically made whole.* [12]

This trauma is evidenced in all manner of shameful, self-defeating self-image/ identities: "I'm not good enough" is then reacted against by the individual and also by their own families and peers in destructive and self-reinforcing ways:

> *Victims of bullying may fall into a vicious circle, where after being victimized, they themselves feel unlovable or incompetent, and their increased low self-esteem is linked to subsequent victimization.* [13]

Nevertheless, I have found that when we impartially allow our feelings to penetrate the pain/body, many benefits

---

[12] Gunnarsson, Nina Veetnisha. (2021) "The Self-perpetuating Cycle of Shame and Self-injury," *Humanity & Society 45*(3): 313.333. https://journals.sagepub.com/doi/pdf/10.1177/0160597620904475

[13] Boungho, Choi, Soowon, Park (2021). "Bullying Perpetration, Victimization, and Low Self-esteem: Examining Their Relationship Over Time," *National Library of Medicine 50*(4): 739-752. https://pubmed.ncbi.nlm.nih.gov/33428081/

come into play. Our feelings, by themselves, create the needed biological, chemical, and genetic changes. As we allow the experience of all of our feelings while remaining *impartial* (Chapter 3, "Nothing Is Personal"), the underlying beliefs triggering these feelings stop being reinforced. As a result, our self-defeating identities and the conditioning associated with them begin to dissolve (Chapter 14, "Feelings"). *This occurs even when we don't entirely know what our beliefs and conditioning are*; we notice our perceptions change, and with them, our relationships change in constructive ways.

It seems that consciousness knows how to orient the mind/body based on the precise information of our "feeling complex" (Chapter 14, "Feelings"). You become more expressive. You gain an understanding and awareness of yourself and your world that you could not acquire in any other way—and in the process, historical trauma is incrementally resolved for yourself and for future generations.

The problem, of course, is fear. How does one face the fear/aversion of observing the negative aspects of their self-image? All creatures are conditioned to run from fear. This book presents seven principles of change that allow one to become incrementally more courageous, open, and present. The more present a person becomes, the more information they take in, and consciousness evolves in surprising and beneficial ways.

Note:

This book is counterintuitive in not telling you how to change. It stresses the opposite because whatever you *do* to change only reinforces inherited perceptions (Chapter 5,

"Whatever You Do To Change Reinforces The Belief That Is Causing Distress"). Instead, this book supports you in aligning with the very forces/phenomena that brought you from the elements to self-awareness: By *impartially* experiencing your feelings/identity/conditioning, you receive awareness you could not obtain under any other circumstance. This awareness, by itself, organically changes you in ways that are tailor-made for you and your world. (Chapter 4, "Consciousness Creates Your Experience, Awareness Changes Consciousness").

Ten premises:

1. Consciousness orients us for optimal benefit.

2. Our feeling complex holds the precise information consciousness requires to orient us, organically and emotionally, to our unique dynamic.

3. As humans became self-aware, they began using thoughts to react against/mitigate unwanted feelings.

4. Reacting against unwanted feelings biases the information consciousness historically used to orient and evolve us in optimal ways.

5. Reacting against unwanted feelings intensifies unresolved trauma in the collective and passes this trauma down to us through succeeding generations.

6. Our self-defeating identities ("I'm not good enough") are directly linked to feelings of humiliation/trauma evaded by past generations.

7. We relate to inherited trauma by *impartially* immersing ourselves in the experience of our feelings—allowing them to speak to the tangible and intangible parts of our pain/body while remaining open to the awareness that arises.

8. The practice of mindful "Noticing" allows us to observe/become aware of our reactions without reinforcing them with another reaction.

9. The less we react, the less we reinforce inherited identities/conditioning (trauma), and the information consciousness uses to orient and evolve us becomes less biased.

10. As we stop reacting to inherited trauma, we stop perpetuating it in ourselves and in future generations.

Definition of terms:

Awareness: Phenomena coalescing into a perception. Webster: *knowledge and understanding that something is happening or exists.*

Overview

Consciousness: The tangible and intangible qualities that create experience and being. Webster says *the state of being characterized by sensation, emotion, volition, and thought: Mind.*

Desire: Using Webster: To express a wish for. Request.

Impartial: Again, I turn to Webster: not partial or *biased: treating or affecting all equally.*

Relativity: Seeing how everything, including yourself, arises out of and receives its form and meaning from everything else. As Webster says, *the state of being dependent for existence on or determined in nature, value, or quality by relation to something else.*

Metaphysics: (Using Merriam-Webster's definition): *A division of philosophy that is concerned with the fundamental nature of reality and being.*

Truth: Again, using Webster: *sincerity in action, character, and utterance.* With one caveat: Everyone's reality is subjective and self-reinforcing. That is, if I'm a bully, bullying will reinforce itself as a requirement to get and keep what I want. However, although I get what I want by bullying, there is an associated truth (dynamic) that says I won't like myself, and my relationships will never be fulfilling. That is to say that every way of being has beneficial as well as detrimental consequences. Nevertheless, as I embrace my truth while remaining open to the possibility that it may not be all that it could be, I think that over time, my truth will change and cohabit rather nicely with your evolving truth as well.

***Self*:** Your evolving personhood.

Chapter 2

Inherited Trauma

When you honestly look, you must accept the possibility that what you have been conditioned to believe about yourself is true.

Chris identified with "I'll never be good enough" because, at least in part, "not good enough" was imprinted into him from conception. "Not good enough" is what one or both of his parents and grandparents felt; he absorbed the feeling/belief while in his mother's womb as chemical reactions to her stresses and joys, the sounds of her world, his parents' relationship. [14] And possibly epigenetically through their sperm and egg:

> *... our experiences, and those of our forebears, are never gone, even if they have been forgotten. They become a part of us, a molecular residue holding fast to*

---

[14] "How Intergenerational Trauma Impacts Families," *Psych Central, Medical Review*, April, 2022: https://psychcentral.com/lib/how-intergenerational-trauma-impacts-families#family-impact

our genetic scaffolding. The DNA remains the same, but psychological and behavioral tendencies are inherited. You might have inherited not just your grandmother's knobby knees, but also her predisposition toward depression caused by the neglect she suffered as a newborn.[15]

After his birth, "not good enough" was a continuation of the conditioning Chris was predisposed to receive; it was part of his parents' attitude toward him—simply because this was their attitude toward themselves.

But then, why was "not good enough" part of Chris's parents' and grandparents' identity? Were they really an inferior breed? A brief review of current and past social relations answers the question quite nicely. When you are oppressed and traumatized, every part of you shuts down—genes are silenced.

Your feelings affect every cell of your body. Under stress, methyl groups, a modifier of gene expression, can attach to cytosine, a chemical base of DNA, creating "epigenetic" changes: Methyl attachments are typically associated with gene silencing—making it harder for a given gene to transcribe its protein. (Reprinted from Chapter 10, "Your Intangible Self")

[15] Hurley, D. (2015). "Grandma's Experiences Leave a Mark on Your Genes," *Discover Magazine* (June 24). https://www.discovermagazine.com/health/grandmas-experiences-leave-a-mark-on-your-genes

When certain genes are silenced, you are less expressive socially and interpersonally.[16] Nurturing works to reverse these effects.[17, 18] Nurturing is associated with food, shelter, grooming—and above all, I think, understanding.

Let's get back to the conditioning Chris's grandparents and their parents' parents received: We all came from humble and traumatic beginnings. Until two hundred years ago, people lived within the constraints of rigid class systems. Wealthy males were the only members of society who enjoyed a semblance of autonomy. Everyone else was dominated or, like surfs, outright owned. For example, an illiterate peasant being subjugated by a feudal lord didn't look him in the eye. Doing so would have been an act of defiance and only invited further subjugation. So, in this scenario, part of Chris's ancestor's conditioning may have been to accept subjugation. Another part of their conditioning may have been to accept humiliation.

Fast forward two hundred or more years, and no one wants to look. Looking creates all manner of consternation; it triggers the phantom fears of punishment that is part of Chris's inherited conditioning. To look, he must not only face the very fears of his ancestors but also question the identity they were forced to accept—an identity they unintentionally affirmed through generations of acquiescence—leaving Chris with the

---

[16] Khazan, Olga (2018). "Inherited Trauma Shapes Your Health," *The Atlantic* (October 16). https://www.bunkhistory.org/resources/inherited-trauma-shapes-your-health

[17] Weaver, I. "Epigenetics in Psychology." https://nobaproject.com/modules/epigenetics-in-psychology

[18] Jones, R. S. (2007). "Reversing the Irreversible." *Nature 450*(7168): 357-9. doi: 10.1038/450357a

fear of not being good enough. It is one thing to counteract your fear with "I am too good enough"—that is what Chris's ancestors did— it is another to face your fear. When you honestly look, you must accept the possibility that what you have been conditioned to believe about yourself is true.

The problem with looking has become even more convoluted. Chris's ancestor had the great bully "lord of the realm" to relate to, but what Chris has is far more nebulous. It includes conditioning communicated through the insensitivities —to a greater or lesser degree— of an abused parent. These insensitivities include all of the irrelevant fears, beliefs, and ways of coping that have evolved to avoid feelings of humiliation—they are essentially prescriptions for getting through life without looking. They have been unwittingly passed down from parent to child for thousands of years—unconsciously reacted against, and thereby reinforced in the collective unconscious. For example, Chris wouldn't have been trying to show that he was "good enough" if he didn't already believe that he was "not good enough." Everything he did to show he was good, only reinforced his belief that he was bad. By the time Chris became self-aware, he was already in conflict with an identity that he inadvertently affirmed through his own efforts to change.

Each feeling contains precise information that is unique to you and your reality; it has a particular edge and shape to it. For example, as a teenager, I became curious about a feeling/fear I had of what I could only describe as the obliterating hand of God. I had no sense that this fear came from the way I was raised by my parents, so I looked to the church.

While I was growing up as the son of a Lutheran minister, I no doubt heard sermons about the righteous hand of God, but I could not sense my dread coming from these sermons. So, I looked to WWII, which was just ending as I was born, but this feeling did not seem to arise from there nor as a holdover from WWI.

Next, I explored the Middle Ages and the hundreds of years of the Catholic Inquisition. Here, I found a match to the edge and shape of my fear: flimsy accusations, coerced confessions, and horrific punishments. The following is a (warning!) very graphic account by Henry Moore of the execution of Lord Bishop Hopper, a protestant condemned by Queen Mary of England in 1555 to burn at the stake:

> *The portly bishop who was in his fifties, stripped to the waist and was affixed to the stake by a single iron band, refusing the two others. The hoop was too short and he had to draw in his stomach to allow the band to be fixed. His paunch hung over the top of it. He had a pound of gunpowder in a bladder in his groin and a pound similarly also under each arm. The man laying the reeds for the pyre asked forgiveness and the bishop told him there was no need. It was his duty and God forgave him. The man then continued to throw up the reeds in a pile about the Lord Bishop. Hooper caught bundles of the reeds and put them too under each arm.*

The command to light the pyre came but it burned poorly, many of the reeds being green. The day was also cold (it was February) and a brisk wind was blowing the flames flat rather than allowing them to rise. Drier tinder was brought and a fiercer fire built causing the gunpowder to flash. Hooper remained alive. In pain, he now prayed in a loud voice: "Lord Jesus, have mercy on me. Lord Jesus, receive my spirit". He continued to repeat these words, the last he ever spoke. Even when his face had completely blackened, and his tongue had swollen so that he could no longer be heard, his lips could be seen moving until they were shrunk to the gums. He began to knock his breast with his hands, but one of his forearms soon fell off, leaving him pummelling <sic> his chest with the other. Fat, water and blood oozed from his finger ends and splashed about with his movements.

More tinder had to be brought as the fire died down. Hooper was losing his strength and he thrust his hand into the iron hoop around his waist. Now the whole of the lower part of his body was burnt away, and then his guts burst out of his paunch, falling over the hoop, and shortly after he keeled over the hoop and fell into the embers, raising a horrified yell from the crowd [7000 onlookers]. It took almost an hour for the bishop to die on the pyre.[19]

[19] Magee, Mike (2006). "The Catholic Inquisition, Methods Of Torture And Victims," *Church and State*, June 1. https://churchandstate.org.uk/2022/06/the-catholic-inquisition-methods-of-torture-and-victims/

Tactics like these allowed the Inquisition to establish a mindset of terror in the citizenry that I believe became incorporated into the collective unconscious. Juan Antonio Llorente (1756-1823), former secretary to the Inquisition, estimates that 32,000 "heretics" were burned at the stake. (Approximately once every two days, during the 200 years of just the Spanish Inquisition.)[20]

> *If the historian includes forms of torture and killing that did not involve a formal trial, along with religious wars and other forms of Catholic violence enacted against Protestants and other non-Catholics (in areas outside of Spain and Portugal), then one can easily speak in terms of millions of people who were killed.*[21]

To be sure, I cannot be certain that my adolescent fear came from cultural trauma created by events like the Inquisition. Nevertheless, finding a historical scenario that so closely matched the edge and shape of my feeling/fear provided the relativity I needed to stop reacting, and my fear faded within weeks.

Imagine living as a peasant during the period of the Inquisition. You would be illiterate, impoverished, and vulnerable. You and your family would be the property of the great lord upon whose land you subsist—to do with as he wished. Your knowledge of the world would be filled with superstitions and fears. In the face of the inquisitor, you would

---

[20] Busentiz, N. "How-many-people-died-in-the-inquisition." https://thecripplegate.com/how-many-people-died-in-the-inquisition/
[21] Ibid.

become very orthodox and faithful. You would become subjective and self-effacing. You would teach your children to not think or question authority. Over time (some 500 years of the European Inquisition), this response becomes conditioned: The conflict and devotion imbued by such historical trauma —good/bad, right/wrong, shame/guilt— can now be evoked by just a word or a symbol. I mention this because, for most of us, our self-image and social orientation evolved from illiterate peasant ancestors; their perception, the product of horrific abuse, created their reality, and their reality reinforced their beliefs down through the ages.

The crime of heresy was not something you did but something you thought. Proving heresy required a confession, and confessions generally required coercion:[22]

> *The inquisitors ... always showed the man or woman the instruments of torture first. These were usually a scourge for flogging, a rack for pulling the limbs until the joints cracked, a strappado and a brasier of burning coals to be applied to bare feet. The strappado was an arrangement by which the victim was suspended, with their hands tied behind their back, by the wrists from the ceiling, and jerked downward if they refused to admit the charge.*[23]

---

[22] *History.com* "Inquisition:" https://www.history.com/topics/religion/inquisition

[23] Magee, Mike (2006). "The Catholic Inquisition, Methods Of Torture And Victims," *Church and State*, June 1. https://churchandstate.org.uk/2022/06/the-catholic-inquisition-methods-of-torture-and-victims/

Any form of evidence could be used against you: trickery, false witness by enemies, witness by children as young as seven, rumors, and anything you or a witness confessed to under torture.

The accused were placed in solitary dungeons for ten or more years to extract confessions. Roman Law, which had governed secular and Church courts prior to the Inquisition was set aside: You were not allowed to know your accusers or the charges brought. You were not allowed to present evidence. Lawyers who defended the accused risked being tried themselves, punished as accomplices, and compelled to disclose information shared by their client.

The Inquisitor was both prosecution and judge. Accused were presumed guilty until proven innocent, and testimony benefited the inquisitor: Evidence retracted, favoring the prosecution, was considered true. Evidence retracted, favoring the defense, was considered perjury and subject to punishment.

Numerous spies and investigators with authority to carry arms and enter homes, together with the Church, secular governments, and entire coerced populations provided inquisitors with evidence.

Interrogations were held in secret. However, the populations of whole towns were compelled to hear the charges brought and witness the execution.

Heretics who confessed had their possessions confiscated. Those who repented were imprisoned for life. Those who merely confessed were burned at the stake. People who had been dead for thirty years were convicted, their bones exhumed and burned, and their families disinherited. [24] Under such horrific abuse, parts of you shut down; you discount inherent wisdom, and you acquiesce to the political spin. Fear, self-doubt, and insensitivity become your way of life.

> *We find in the civil law of today many evidences of inquisitorial origin.* [25]

So, while it is important to recount the injustice and heroism of your ancestors, it is vital that you remain sensitive to the information contained in your unique feelings; because unacknowledged trauma can create conflicts that you unconsciously react against, and these reactions have a way of recreating the original injury in yourself and your decedents. (Wolynn, Chapter 9, "You Must Become The Impartial Observer Of Yourself")

---

[24] Scott, J. G. "Trial Methods of the Inquisition," p. 3-10. https://digitalcommons.du.edu/cgi/viewcontent.cgi?article=6997&context=dlr

[25]. Ibid.

Chapter 3

The First Principle:

Nothing Is Personal

If there is a lot of turbulence, you are mostly cloudy; less turbulence, and you have sunnier days.

Kim felt she didn't fit in and, as a result, was anxious in social situations, but the more carefully she orchestrated how she would relate, the less she seemed to resonate. That is, the more Kim reacted against what she didn't like about herself, the more she reinforced what she did not like. However, the better Kim became at identifying her reactions —the "I do not fit in" self-talk of her wounded inner child— the less influence her inherited identity had over her. She could no longer reinforce her belief by reacting against it— tensing up whenever someone spoke to her and responding with a self-effacing laugh. She found even greater relativity when she tied her social dissonance (conditioned reaction) to her childhood experience of being excluded from family interactions (the source of her conditioning). As inherited beliefs stopped being reinforced (reacted against), a new Kim emerged—someone she enjoyed as she integrated more and more with her social circle—someone she could have never known to be.

The problem with awareness of ourselves, though, is that it can so easily be biased by our natural desire to see ourselves in a positive light. To identify her reactions, Kim needed a platform from which she could observe herself with ruthless objectivity—even explore the possibility that she had unwittingly identified with more negativity than she actually had—to know the extent of it; that is, I'm this empathetic/ supportive /understanding, but not that. I am this angry/anxious/depressed, but not that. I am this addicted/perverted/corrupt, but not that. Kim had to dare to look, to know where she began and ended, to find what motivated her to do and be what she was: What were her influencers and triggers—who or what was driving her bus?

For myself, I have to know my parameters to orient and mature. At the same time, I have to know that whatever I discover about myself, particularly what I do not appreciate, has nothing to do with who I am. It has to do with the abuse and nurturing that I arose from. The more impartially I observe my dysfunction, the better able I am to separate from it.

The First Principle:

Nothing in life —even who you have come to see yourself to be— is personal. [26]

[26] Leiby, John Samuel. *The Unpublished Lectures, 1978-1995.*

Nothing Is Personal

What a statement! You might want to stop here, light a candle, or walk around the block to reflect on this concept. Not even you have anything personal to do with how you have come to see yourself. It is important to realize that your beliefs, attitudes, and even the conditioning you create, and in many ways perpetuate, have nothing to do with you and who you are.

The way I integrate this "nothing personal" principle is to see my identity and associated behavior as the product of an energy dynamic: A dynamic of largely unconscious, mechanical, self-reinforcing reactions to my fears and the fears and beliefs I unknowingly inherited from my parents, and their parent's parents. Take a moment to reflect on how your feelings, attitudes, and conditioned reactions may interrelate to reinforce and perpetuate a harmful belief/identity.

This energy dynamic that incorporates my identity interrelates with another energy dynamic from which my supportive and self-defeating beliefs evolved. This is the mindset/consciousness of the social structure. The social structure contains all the unresolved fears, attitudes, and beliefs created by all the belligerence, lies, truths, and catastrophes experienced since life began. This dynamic has been unconsciously passed down through the generations from time immemorial … to me.

I am a phenomenon made up of my genetics, plus whatever mix of sanity and insanity I've inherited from the abuses and nurturing of the social structure. John Leiby said: *Your experience is subject to the same laws of physics that cause clouds to appear and then vanish in a clear blue sky.*[27] If there is a lot of turbulence, you are mostly cloudy; less turbulence, and you have sunnier days. Your experience is the product of a social consciousness that existed long before you came into being and will continue long after you are gone.

Figure 1. *Your Involvement in the chaotic energy of the social structure: As you impartially allow your feelings while observing the discordant influences of your world, you Become increasingly defined/relative.*

How do you separate from trauma that has been knitted to you through your mother's fears from conception? How, at age twelve, for example, when you are just beginning to think logically [28]—when the identity you've inherited conflicts with *you*? How do you resolve that you are not worthless when the evaluation you've incorporated from the abuses of the social structure says that you are?

The problem with self-exploration is fear; all creatures are conditioned to run from fear. Questioning self-defeating beliefs that we have simultaneously been conditioned not to question is frightening and confusing. Rather than

[27] Leiby, John Samuel. *The Unpublished Lectures, 1978-1995.*
[28] Stanford Children's Health/Lucile Packard Children's Hospital. "Cognitive Development in the Teen Years."

questioning, we counteract: "God tells me I am not worthless." As humans became self-aware, we began creating thoughts/beliefs to counteract/mitigate unwanted feelings instead of relating to them. Carl Hoffman gives an account of the mindset of New Guinea stone-age head-hunting Asmat tribes in the Mid 1950's:

> *The Asmat lived in a complex world of spirits kept in balance by elaborate ceremonies and constant reciprocal violence. No death just happened. Even sickness came at the hand of the spirits. Every villager could see them, talk to them. There were spirits in the rattan and in the mangrove and sago trees, in the whirlpools, in their own fingers and noses. There was their world, and there was the world of the Safan, the realm of the souls and kingdom of the ancestors across the seas. The worlds were equally real, sickness and death kept in check by constant appeasement and scaring of the spirits of their ancestors back to beyond the sea where they belonged, where they could do no harm.* [29]

Asmat beliefs shaped their reality, and their reality reinforced their beliefs —an airplane was interpreted as "*opndettaji—a passing-over-canoe-of-the-spirits*."[30] I recall an excerpt in which a New Guinea tribal member asked a

[29] Hoffman, Carl (2014). *Savage Harvest: A Tale of Cannibals, Colonialism and Michael Rockefeller's Tragic Quest for Primitive Art,* William Morrow and Co. p.33. Carl Hoffman, *Savage Harvest: A Tale of Cannibals, Colonialism and*
[30] Ibid

European, "How is it that you have guns and helicopters, and we have arrows and spears?" All of the advances that we, in the modern world, credit ourselves for having derived from a few individuals; Copernicus, for example, who, in 1543, faced his fear of the Catholic Inquisition, posited that the earth revolves around the sun, and launched the scientific revolution.[31]

Thoughts evolved from feelings, so feelings can trigger thoughts and thoughts can trigger feelings. Thoughts are codified feelings. You tell yourself/believe that you're unlovable because you feel unlovable. As a result, we have developed all manner of emotional regulatory systems in the form of thoughts to counteract/misdirect —lie about— dreadful, conflicting feelings. Every emotional regulatory system that has ever been developed works; that is, it counteracts/mitigates unwanted feelings: We say, in so many words and deeds, "I am too lovable." In so doing, we bias the information consciousness historically used to orient and evolve us optimally. Consider the possibility that all reactions and many beliefs, thoughts, and behaviors are emotional regulatory systems.

You could say this is just me talking; however, any attempt to challenge an emotional regulatory system is met with an immediate visceral, often hostile reaction. It is not that we're not evolving; it is just that our evolution is biased by whatever emotional regulatory system we use. We have,

---

[31] Riebeek, H. (2009). "The History of an Idea That Launched the Scientific Revolution," *Planetary Motion.* https://earthobservatory.nasa.gov/features/OrbitsHistory

perhaps, become technologically intelligent at the expense of emotional intelligence. A possible effect is that we now evolve to a greater extent along predetermined lines, as opposed to the organic, improbable, and creative changes that resulted in a naked, self-aware human.

A helpful way of observing your conditioned reactions is to "notice" them. When you react, you reinforce conditioning; however, noticing allows awareness while mitigating your reaction. The act of noticing is neutral: I have gum on my shoe — "Isn't that interesting;" "I wonder how it got there." It could have been me, a friend, or a distant relative thoughtlessly tossing their gum. Until I become relative to it, I'll leave gum-prints everywhere I go. To become relative to your inherited trauma, you must observe yourself impartially—what you see that you are and what you see that you are not—so that consciousness can orient around the truth of it. The process of "orienting and becoming relative" is the process of separating out from your conditioning.

Truthfulness is essential. You have to be with (experience) what you believe yourself to be without reacting—that is, without trying to escape or mitigate your inherited identity—and without taking it personally. Experiencing/grieving every nuance of your identity—what you see yourself to be, what you have done, and what was done to you—allows consciousness to orient around and become relative to it. (See Chapter 15, "Grief")

As stated, reacting reinforces your belief, whereas neutrality allows it to be affirmed, altered, or dissipated into irrelevance; what remains is a greater appreciation of your essential self. In addition, you must be fair and evenhanded in your relationships: Deceit, connivance, and outright theft … create the very trauma dynamic that drives dysfunction in yourself and others—it corrupts the phenomena out of which you arise.

As you stay with your truth, integrity builds, and with it, identity and definition; awareness feeds back upon itself, building upon your evolving appreciation of what is. Each time you notice how you are not neutral, you incrementally become more neutral.

Returning to the example at the beginning of this Chapter, Kim had to become her own scientific experiment to get relative to her "I do not fit in" thinking. She had to impartially observe what Kim does—allowing herself to be whatever she was—and then look for what motivated her to be what she was without contaminating the evidence with a defensive reaction. The attitude of *noticing* helped Kim become aware of the nuances of her reactions without taking them personally. She had to discover: "What does my doing do?" The more Kim understood, the less she reacted and the less she reinforced inherited trauma.

It's your reactions that reinforce your reality. It's awareness of your reactions that changes your perception. Using Chris's example from Chapter 2, by just acknowledging that he was trying to be "good enough" because he believed he was "not good enough," Chris changed. He couldn't spend another moment reinforcing his "not good enough" identity by reacting against it. Both beliefs, good and not good enough, suddenly became irrelevant, and Chris experienced a more harmonious reality.

Each time you notice, you change—just a little. Each time you change, you notice more. Even noticing that you are not noticing adds awareness and allows new pathways to develop. Over a brief time, you will notice yourself staying with what is with greater consistency.

There are numerous principles, awareness, and skills that each of us must incorporate to face our fear and separate from the trauma of the social structure. This book identifies seven helpful ones: They are like the push I received on my bicycle as a child, which taught me balance. Each chapter expands upon the last, building toward a unified concept of organic change: Rather than remembering how to be or what to do, you become it; you incrementally become the person who inherently knows.

Chapter 4

The Second Principle:

Consciousness Creates Your Experience, Awareness Changes Consciousness

Observing your unvarnished self,
changes you into how you should be.

Brook hated the seven-to-five grind of her job and commute. To offset her feelings, she took a moment to make an attitude adjustment before she started her day; but when Brook made an attitude adjustment, she biased the subtle information life was giving her about herself and the dynamic engulfing her. However, as she impartially allowed herself to experience her feelings, they spoke to her about her life: what she was doing, why she was doing it, her fears, and defenses—how she came to be as she was. Brook could only allow her feelings to engulf her by being very clear:

Consciousness Creates Your Experience, Awareness Changes Consciousness

Nothing in life —even who you have come to see yourself to be— is personal.[32]

As Brook allowed awareness of the many nuances of her attitude—the feelings, beliefs, identities, and dynamics out of which all of these arose—her attitude began to change. The change wasn't anything she could have picked out of a hat, like deciding to be kinder or more cheerful. She may have attempted to describe it, but she would have never been able to put it into words completely. Like her, her new attitude is indefinable and always evolving—integrating and varying with her being and life dynamic. The process of *impartially* noticing what her attitude is and why, incrementally moves Brook toward greater integrity, courage, and self-sufficiency. She knows more of who she is and what she is about; this knowledge reduces stress and motivates constructive decisions.

Many counselors will tell you, for example, that grateful people live longer, happier lives and that we should, therefore, practice gratitude. But you cannot arbitrarily change your attitude without conflicting yourself. Your attitude arose out of an energy dynamic. How do you change your attitude without changing the dynamic it evolved from? How do you change a dynamic that is the product of everything else?

You may decide, for example, that you need to be more loving and, as a result, organize "Sandwiches for The Homeless." But if you are not more loving now—if love is not

---

[32] Leiby, John Samuel. *The Unpublished Lectures, 1978-1995.*

emanating from you of its own accord, if love is not your natural state—then you do not know what "being more loving" is. What others experience when you project "love"—the dissociation, confusion, and cynicism—are anything but loving. The homeless eat your sandwich along with their cynicism, which only works to keep them homeless. This is the fragility of the energy engulfing you: When you arbitrarily change your behavior, you fragment your world and yourself.

All you can do, and this is the theme at the heart of this work, is "notice" what your attitude is and the influences contributing to it. As you allow awareness about your attitude, you will notice that your attitude will begin to change. As your attitude evolves, you relate differently to your dynamic, and your dynamic begins to relate differently to you. (See Chapter 11, "Active Non-Doing")

Each time you notice you have an attitude about this or that, each time you notice what your attitude does, an incremental change occurs. New pathways develop as old ones fade. As you see your attitude more clearly—why it is as it is and what it does—it begins to change. It has to because awareness adds to consciousness, and consciousness —the source from which we all arise— feeds back upon awareness, continuously expanding and becoming something other.

Change is effortless because it's not *you* creating it. The change is not something you can predetermine. How can you know the required change (what "more loving" is) when you have never experienced it? The change cannot come from platitudes, affirmations, or willpower. How you think you should be has nothing to do with the subtleties of the dynamics shaping you; it has nothing to do with who *you* are. It is the opposite: Observing your unvarnished self, changes you into how you should be.

The problem, though, is with noticing your attitude and being curious about it. Why, for example, would you be curious about your need to "be more loving" when projecting love deludes you into seeing yourself as more caring and constructive than you naturally are? Why would you notice an attitude that helps you ignore aspects of yourself that you do not like? Moreover, why would you become curious about your acts of so-called kindness when they are the one thing you can do and not be criticized for?

That's why walking around the block a time or two while *impartially* reflecting upon this energy dynamic that you are is so important. The self-defeating aspects of your attitude evolved out of fear, and you will never allow yourself to see your fear (Chapter 23, "Subjective Reality") if you are always defending yourself against it.

Chapter 5

The Third Principle:

Whatever You Do To Change Reinforces The Belief That Is Causing Distress

Doing is the trap that drives dysfunction.

The text of the Heart Sutra likely originated in southern India. It was translated into Chinese around AD 250 by the Buddhist monk Chih-ch'ien. The title for the text, though, didn't appear until Hsuan Tsan's translation in AD 649. The Heart Sutra speaks to the fundamental nature of phenomena. The text comprises some thirty lines that revolve around the following seven:

Form is emptiness, emptiness is form;
emptiness is not separate from form,
form is not separate from emptiness;
whatever is form is emptiness,
whatever is emptiness is form.
The same holds for sensation and perception,
memory and consciousness. [33]

The first Sutra: *Form is emptiness; emptiness is form*, may sound like a discussion of quantum physics; however, the classic interpretation is that everything in the universe arises out of and receives its form and meaning from everything else in the universe.

As Thich Nhat Hanh states, "Without a cloud, there will be no rain; without rain, the trees cannot grow; and without trees, we cannot make paper."[34] We are, therefore, dependent upon the factors that cause us to be as we are. Consequently, you and I, and everything else, are "empty of separate or independent selves."[35] The concept of good arises out of the concept of bad. Neither concept can exist independently of the other.

---

[33] Pine, R. *The Heart Sutra,* Counterpoint, 2004. p. 2.

[34] Thích Nhất Hạnh ."The Heart Sutra: The Fullness of Emptiness." *Lion's Roar.* September 16, 2022. https://www.lionsroar.com/heart-sutra-fullness-emptiness/

[35] "Prajnaparamita (Heart) Sutra." https://www.purifymind.com/HeartSutraPra.htm

Whatever You Do To Change Reinforces The Belief That Is Causing Distress

The Sutra continues: *emptiness is not separate from form, form is not separate from emptiness*. When you pursue self-love to avoid self-hatred, you must realize that the meaning of these words arises out of and in opposition to the other. They relate to the same phenomena, feelings, and fears.

In this example, self-love and self-hatred are metaphysically the same. Everything you do to feel good about yourself only reinforces the self-image you are trying to counteract. You look for ways to love yourself because you dislike or even hate yourself. The truth is, there would be no motive to pursue self-love if you knew what self-love was.

When you project some desperate fantasy that you envision to be the opposite of what you are experiencing, all you achieve is a reflection of what you are experiencing. This means that the pursuit of self-love is just a euphemism for self-hatred. Your reaction against what you are is within the realm of who you are. The latte you bought to soothe, comfort, and reward yourself only reinforces the belief that is causing distress.

Taking this one step further, everything you pursue manifests as its opposite. If you pursue beauty, you get ugliness—or a form of it. If you pursue goodness, you get evil. When you pursue heaven, you achieve hell. While this may sound like Orwellian doublethink, it is true if you think about it. People who pursue power are imprisoned in compounds, surrounded by armed guards: Literally thousands of secret service agents precede and surround the U.S. presidents.[36]

---

[36] "13 ways Secret Service agents keep the president safe when he travels," *The Oregonian*. May 7, 2015

Those who pursue wealth can be emotionally impoverished, relying on social position for identity and meaning. Paul J. Getty (once the wealthiest man in the world) refused ransom for his grandson until it was reduced to the deductible amount for his income tax.[37] Those looking for ways to love themselves have been among the most unforgiving. Christina Crawford's account of Joan Crawford in Mommy Dearest speaks of a vindictive, self-serving narcissist who is dependent upon others for self-adoration.[38] And the pursuit of peace appears to manifest as endless war: As of this notice (January 2025) the United States has been at peace for 17 years out of the 249 years of its existence. [39]

If what you have just read makes sense, you are beginning to appreciate the conflict and insanity arising from the struggle "to be a better person." Not only is there no way of knowing what is needed to feel good about yourself, whatever is done is just another version of this self that you are trying to improve. Doing is the trap that drives dysfunction.

The Sutra concludes: *The same holds for sensation and perception, memory and consciousness.* Jordan Peterson, psychology professor, author, and public speaker, states: "If

---

https://www.oregonlive.com/politics/2015/05/13_ways_secret_service_agents.html

[37] Scott, Ridley (2024). "*The Life of I. Paul Getty, the 'richest man in the history of the world.'" Gentleman's Journal*, December 12. https://www.thegentlemansjournal.com/article/life-j-paul-getty-richest-man-history-world

[38] Crawford, Christina. *Mommy Dearest*, William Morrow and Co, 1978

[39] Carpenter, Arthur (2017). "The U.S. Has Been At War 222 out of 239 Years," *Hypotheses Freakonometrics*. March. https://freakonometrics.hypotheses.org/50473

you lie to yourself and others, you corrupt the structure that you use to interact with being."[40] Lying degenerates every aspect of a relationship: sensitivity, empathy, understanding, intimacy, connection, trust, emotional stability… You will never understand why you do what you do—or develop a sense of who you are and what you are about—without the intention to be true.

One caveat: The intention of becoming "aware" to change your self-image reinforces the self-image/reality you are trying to change: The change you seek is within the context of who you are. Therefore, everything you do to change only reinforces the self you are working to improve. It is more of doing this to get that—more of emptiness being form and form being emptiness, creating peace by making war.

The solution is *noticing*—consistently noticing how you are acting with motive moves you in the direction of less and less motive. It becomes an attitude more like a plant turning toward sunlight than the calculus of getting this by doing that. As you observe yourself changing in surprising ways, you become more and more interested in what is, "truth;" you care less and less about how you want to be and more about understanding the phenomena shaping you.

---

[40] Peterson, J. *The Necessity of Virtue.* https://www.youtube.com/watch?v=Nvm-ysHB3es

Whatever You Do To Change Reinforces The Belief That Is Causing Distress

However you feel about yourself is a product of the people and conditions you are in relation to. You arose organically and unconsciously out of these conditions. You cannot change how you feel about yourself any more than a cloud can choose to appear or not appear in the sky. If you think you are "bad," you cannot make yourself think you are "good." The more you try to look good, the more you reinforce the mindset of good versus bad and all the parameters that give your perception validity.

Selflessness, for example, can be a virtue, but trying to be selfless is just a form of pseudo-piety, which is hypocrisy. Hypocrisy triggers reactions in others, such as cynicism and resentment. These reactions to our hypocrisy impede our progress and that of everyone around us—preventing the experience of the moment.

However, if you notice all of the ways you deviate from presence—how you are insincere, inconsiderate, or create disruption—you will become increasingly selfless, among many other things. It is interesting to note that none of the virtues arising from being with what is have anything to do with the moment you are noticing. More significantly, none of these virtues have anything to do with achieving anything.

Awareness added to consciousness = change.

As I impartially observe myself—allowing my feelings and fears and noticing when they are too overwhelming—new thoughts and perceptions arise; these perceptions are directly linked to what I can be with. What I can be with shapes the phenomena out of which my perceptions arise—I couldn't experience them under any other circumstance. These new awarenesses are ever more truthful in that they successively build upon what I see in myself that is not neutral, impartial, or true. This is how just 5% of "being with," even if it is only glimpsing at how I might have been unconstructive, evolves into magnitudes greater understanding than the attitude of 100% evasion. The more impartial I become, the less I manipulate those around me to feel better about myself; the underlying dynamic/belief, the "I'm not good enough," stops being reacted against, so it stops being reinforced and fades into irrelevance.

> *Incremental noticing creates incrementally greater neutrality.*

Since everything arises out of and receives its form and meaning from everything else, allowing what is balances everything out. As you become increasingly neutral, you understand more and more why things and people are as they are. You empathize with the self-perpetuating dynamic everyone is caught in—how we feed into and reinforce the others' position/reality. You stop blaming, reacting, and biasing—you mature, stabilize, and find meaning.

Understanding that everything in the universe arises out of everything else supports the notion that whatever you do not like about yourself has nothing to do with you; it has to do with the dynamics within and around you. You are living out the equation:

Whatever You Do To Change Reinforces The Belief That Is Causing Distress

Trauma + awareness = maturity.

It is a law of physics that water boils at 212 °F. Similarly, like it or not, under certain conditions, you will do things that are harmful to you. Acting out is always an unconscious reaction—all you can do is stay with the experience and allow the feelings resulting from the fallout of your reaction to inform consciousness. Whatever awareness you allow about yourself and your world reshapes you; it changes the parameters of the phenomenon from which you arise. You become the person who used to vaporize under such and such conditions but now does not. The definitions and stigma that have channeled you onto unconstructive paths become more irrelevant as you become increasingly neutral.

You became who you are organically and unconsciously. Your mother's attitude and the tension of her world are incorporated into every fiber of your being. As you developed, you interpreted your (self-defeating) feelings as, for example, "I am hopelessly defective." Being defective may not be the specific identity that you relate to, but whatever it is, you will not undo it with logic. You will not undo it with affirmations and mantras. You will not undo it by counteracting what you do not like about yourself. You will not undo it by taking deep breaths and remembering what not to think and do. You will not undo it because whatever you do is just another version of the self you are trying to change.

The undoing then comes from beyond the mind. Call it consciousness, God, source, the intelligence from which you were formed. Whatever you look to must be that which brought you from the elements and carried you to the present day, that which creates change on the organic, elemental, chemical, and cellular levels. Change so minute—so in the moment—you cannot put it into words. It is preverbal, unconscious change without intention.

Chapter 6

The Fourth Principle: Truth Is The Foundation Of Being

Every awareness you allow adds wisdom.

Being in inner space is a lot like being in outer space: there are no anchors —nothing to ground you— up is down, or sideways, there is no direction. If you wish to connect with some other celestial being, you must orient around a moving target. When some influence sets you into a tilt/spin/tumble/orbit bias, you could tilt/spin/orbit forever. Only, if you do not learn to objectively reflect, you may never become aware that you are tilting/spinning/orbiting; quite likely, you may never become aware of what it is that you are orbiting around. You could be spinning, but believe that you are still and that everyone/thing else is orbiting around you—that you are the center of the universe. Someone/thing else could be tilted, but because they/it is more influential, you may come to believe that you are tilted; seeing yourself as tilted is painful and frightening, so you could consciously or unconsciously form beliefs, practices, points of logic, and conditioned reactions that support the illusion that you are aligned. Numerous physical laws govern your relationship in inner and outer space so that every position, from your perspective (tilt/spin/tumble/orbit bias), is correct (Chapter 23, "Subjective Reality"). The only aligning principle is the awareness that arises from your intention to be true.

If one part of your being is biased, every part of your being is biased. To observe yourself impartially, you must find a place to stand that is new and unbiased, a place in you that has not been conditioned by either yourself or the social structure. You find this place by being as truthful as you know how to be with yourself, everyone else, and everything else:

> *Your intention of truthfulness creates an evolving contradiction between what existed previously and your arising self.* [41]

Each time you notice how you were not present—insincere or reactive—an incremental change occurs in the direction of presence, sincerity, and understanding. Every change has a multidimensional effect that reflects upon awareness and adds to consciousness. You need to do nothing more than be with what is and notice when you are not.

Being with what is adds awareness to consciousness, awareness changes consciousness. When consciousness changes, you change. As you change, the evolving contradiction

[41] Hoefer, David. L. "Conditioning."

created by noticing what is more true creates a new you who is less biased, less conditioned, and more relative than you were a millisecond earlier. This is how consciousness builds upon itself.

It is impossible to create an evolving contradiction around an "I want." What I want is based on fantasy, guesswork, and a desire for distraction. There is nothing real or consistent to refer to, no foundation to build upon. "I want" reinforces conditioning and inherited beliefs—it takes you in circles.

The evolving contradiction can only arise out of being with what is, what you are experiencing now. You can only build upon what you see that you are or were not: "I was not as present, courteous, poised, appreciative as I now see that I could have been." Give this awareness to consciousness. Let consciousness fill in the blind spots and repair the broken pieces.

Your appreciation of what integrates and what disintegrates your sense of self directs your understanding of what is true. For example, I was conflicted over my promise to a friend: I feared becoming enmeshed in a co-dependent relationship. So, I went against my promise; I honored my feelings and lost my friend. Afterward, I noticed that I felt more integrated and more in touch with who I am. The truer you are, the less biased you become and the greater the contradiction between who you are now and what existed previously.

You can observe the change from your reaction: You can see that you reacted —or gave yourself away— this much, but not as much as you have in the past. Seeing how you were childish allows you to mature; every awareness you allow adds wisdom. You can observe the change in your connection to others, your emotional stability, and your sense of self—you know that what you once were, you will never be again.

Chapter 7

The Fifth Principle:

Meaning Arises Out Of The Relationship Between Form And Emptiness

Whatever space you allow, allows meaning to arise out of it.

If everything were form, there would be no emptiness. If everything were emptiness, there would be no form (*The Heart Sutra*, Chapter 5). Form arises out of emptiness as emptiness arises out of form. Out of the relationship between form and emptiness comes meaning.

Paraphrasing Lao Tsu in the *Tao Te Ching*: "You build a house, but the meaning arises from the space between its walls. You shape clay into a pot, but the meaning arises from the emptiness inside." [42] You read this page, but the meaning arises from the space between words. Continuing my paraphrase: "We work at being, but the meaning of it arises [out of stillness —when we are empty— often, doing nothing.at all. As Lao Tsu says] from non-being."

[42] Mitchell, Stephen / Lao Tsu, *Tao Te Ching,* Harper & Row, 1988. p.11.

Meaning Arises Out Of The Relationship Between Form And Emptiness

Meaning arises from inner space in a similar way: With every interaction, energy coalesces, expands, contracts, changes density, and forms anew; new patterns of flow are created, not only from within but from without. The shape and flow of cities arise as interrelationships with inner space that incrementally structure the culture and ideas of its creators. That is, as thinking becomes rigid, we become traumatized; we constrict, and the patterns of meaning become enmeshed; they become form as opposed to fluid relationships between form and emptiness.

John Leiby (Acknowledgement) spoke of the space needed for meaning to arise using the example of the space required between cars —at least six car lengths— while driving the freeway to maneuver and be safe; other drivers, seeing the space he had created, would take it up by merging or passing; so, he continually found himself in a state of "moving forward by falling back." The principle applies to every aspect of being: introspection, relations, economics, and creativity. Depending upon the conditions, a given amount of space (courtesy or time laps—sometimes years) is required to relate to one another, ourselves, and other things. John recalled one incident where he used the race-car driving skills of his youth —alternately breaking while turning the wheel to slide from side to side and then accelerating— to avoid collisions with oncoming cars spinning and tumbling out of control in an interstate pile-up.

People who have been in automobile accidents have reported the impending collision occurring in slow motion. Consciousness seems to have sped up like a high-speed camera depicting the convulsive explosion of a bullet fired through a cube of gelatin. The truth is that consciousness records the complexity of every moment to this same degree. However, I think that, in shielding ourselves from painful feelings, we close off the space through which the subtleties (meaning) of life arise. We become like high-speed bumper-to-bumper drivers—clueless about why we never saw such and such disaster coming.

Where do you find the maturity to relate to life? Within the wonderment is the space required for meaning to arise. The courage and skill needed to look impartially arise from the space created by simply noticing and allowing awareness of how you see that you are not courageous or skillful. The more open you are to your shortcomings, the more space you allow and the less you react. The less you react, the less reinforcement self-defeating beliefs and conditioning receive, and the quicker they lose influence. As they lose influence, you orient differently as your world orients differently around this new you; you experience more spontaneity, and self-defeating reactions decrease. Like a word between the spaces, you take on meaning: You identify patterns and phenomena; you see what's coming because there is a separate you to see it.

When caught between a shameful identity and your logic, it is easy to become confused. That is, if I feel stupid and act stupid, then I must be stupid. But how do I find out if I am stupid when the thought is a stigma that I react against, and my reaction suggests it is true? How do I discover if I am stupid when thoughts trigger fears and fears reinforce beliefs? How do I discover if I am stupid when everyone and everything in my world says it is true? How do I observe myself impartially? How do I allow myself to be?

Caught in the belief, I have no way of knowing. I can only be with how I see myself now without adding to or subtracting from the dynamic engulfing me. I do this by simply noticing, "I'm feeling really stupid right now—isn't that interesting?" I stay with the feeling and the awareness that arises. What may come to mind is that someone in my world said something reminiscent of the criticism I received from a parent. My next observation may be that I am tripping all over myself, trying to show myself and others that I am really brilliant and how stupid that effort makes me feel.

The whole time, I stay with my feelings, not reacting and carefully noticing when and how I do react; I add space. The parts of my identity that require reinforcement —that I inherited from the social structure— fall away. The essence that is the evolving me, the part that was smart enough to know (if) I did something stupid, remains.

You sustain false realities with your resistance. Resistance eliminates space and cuts off awareness; that is, whatever you do to create space/meaning is what fills it up. For example, everything you do to prove yourself acceptable closes space. Allowing the possibility that you are not acceptable opens it.

Allowing the possibility that you are not acceptable is the exact opposite of what you have been doing. It is the exact opposite of what is needed to insulate yourself from feelings of shame and guilt and to keep from triggering feelings of troublesome beliefs, such as "I'm not good enough." That's why, before you observe yourself objectively —to see your shortcomings— you must be well-grounded in:

> *Nothing in life —even who you have come to see yourself to be— is personal.*[43]

Your identity developed under certain conditions. It has a particular shape and quality to it, like a stamp engraved with the unique abuse you suffer; for the most part, it exists in the preverbal realm of consciousness, and only you can touch it (Chapter 10, "Your Intangible Self," and Chapter 14, "Feelings"). As you allow the pain of it to teach you—how you fumble, how you came to be as you are, the rough edges that catch on this and that, that trip and trigger you—you are adding space. Learn about the exclusive dynamic engulfing you: your pain, conditioning, and fear. The particular feelings related to the occurrence and inherent quality of your suffering contain the precise wisdom life/consciousness requires to connect you to yourself and your world. The maturity and answers arise out of the space created by being with what is.

Maria felt abandoned by Robert, who was spending more of his weekends in the garage. This lack of attention triggered her "I'm unlovable" fear, and she began withdrawing and then lashing out at Robert with recriminations. However, as Maria

[43] Samuel, John. *The Unpublished Lectures.*

embraced her feeling —by noticing, "Isn't it interesting that I believe myself to be unlovable?"— she was led to the origins of her fear.

As Maria allowed the experience of her fear, she discredited its underlying belief (even when she did not entirely know what that belief was). She also acclimated to her fear instead of reinforcing it by running from it or trying to get Robert to relate to her differently. Reflecting on her early life and how she came to see herself as she did gave her perspective. Noticing how she reacted added relativity to the origins of self-defeating beliefs and allowed her to react less. The less she reacted, the less she reinforced her belief. As "unlovable" faded, she began relating person to person. Person to person, she saw her value. Everything needed to free her —seeing that her self-image had nothing to do with who she was— was hiding in what is. "Unlovable" became irrelevant.

As Maria became aware of how she did not see herself as a person, she began to see herself as a person. That is how consciousness works. It evolves out of impartially being with (embracing) your shortcomings and self-defeating beliefs instead of trying to overcome them. Do you see how noticing that she was not neutral about this or that moved Maria toward neutrality? Do you see how being neutral toward herself worked to dissolve the stigma of her self-image? Do you see how trying to overcome was an evasion while noticing her shortcomings was relating directly to the injury or condition that needed attention?

Whatever space you allow,
allows meaning to arise out of it.

Chapter 8

The Sixth Principle:

Change Is Organic, Unconscious And The Product Of Minute Energy Vibrations

Each time you notice an influence
affecting the way you walk through life,
your walk changes.

Move your hand, and you move your wrist and arm. The muscles around your chest and back tense ever so slightly; your head turns just a little, your neck and spine adjust in counterbalance, your hips and legs reposition, and your feet ground you. In short, every part of you moves your hand. Then, if you look at the way your hand moves, with grace or in defense, you will see that it is your relationship with yourself and your world that moves your hand. As you observe this relationship and how it came to be as it is, you see that it was the acceptance or abuse that your parents and your parents' parents received that moves your hand.

Change Is Organic Unconscious And The Product Of Minute Energy Vibrations

Each time you notice an influence affecting the way you walk through life, your walk changes; you react a little less to inherited conditioning, and you become less affected, more spontaneous—and more present. In presence, you become increasingly sensitive to the influence of influences. This is not so much a thinking process but rather a sensing process. A "being with" process—allowing what is to coalesce into greater understanding. Understanding arises from your involvement while relating to the phenomena you are a part of; it does not come from the phenomenon; it does not come from thinking; it is a new creation, a culmination of energies.

At first, "being with" may be painful. How you see yourself may not align with what you do. However, what you do is what you have become. Feeling the humiliation of not aligning with your self-image creates change on every level of consciousness. When you allow the experience of what is true, every part of you resonates.

Your perception of change shapes your change. For example, if you see change as a continuous exertion of willpower, that is what you will experience. You may also miss critical transitions. You may, for example, stop drinking but never resolve the fear and injury that drinking anesthetized. If you see change arising out of beliefs and practices, your beliefs and practices will prove themselves invaluable as you become more and more your definition of loving, more and more your definition of virtue.

But if you see change as an organic process informed by awareness, you will have no idea what you are becoming. The only thing shaping you will be your awareness of what it is that you are being with: What you see that you are being with alters your perception of what is true, as that truth alters your perception of what you are being with. As the truth of things becomes increasingly defined, you begin to appreciate the multitude of infinitesimal transactions required for growth and healing—the complexity of being.

One gigantic step may seem daunting, but an infinitesimally small step is effortless. Just acknowledging that you are being self-defeating begins the process. Just staying with this knowing adds to awareness; it is a matter of allowing the next awareness and the next while experiencing your dynamic and fear. You discover that it is not you that changes you, but rather your awareness of you and your world that changes you. As you change, you begin to see with ever-increasing clarity the world you have arisen out of and the injury that you have suffered, and for a time, you feel more pain; at this point, you must know within yourself (trust) that this "source" that brought you from the elements to self-awareness will continue to evolve you in optimal and surprising ways.

What you are becoming expresses itself in trillions of infinitesimal units of information at the fringes of awareness. You can sense this, though you will never grasp it completely. It is indescribable. Nevertheless, as you attend to these sensations, consciousness is better able to organize around the parts of yourself that you cannot verbalize or even comprehend. These sensations are the headwaters of how you see yourself and what you understand. What you understand and how you understand it shapes cognitive experience; it picks and chooses your relationships; it orients you to yourself and your dynamic.

Your feelings are unique to you. They are profoundly dense and precise forms of information that relate to every aspect of your world (Chapter 14, "Feelings"). Let them speak to the conscious as well as unconscious parts of you. Allow them to orient you around what is tangible as well as intangible. Reflect upon the perceptions that arise from "being with." They may be sane or insane. With all the lies and manipulation, there are many ways to become misguided, many reasons for acting crazy. Each time you acknowledge a conflict, internal or external, you become a little truer. Every perception is a change; every change has a multidimensional effect—affecting not only every aspect of you but everything else. As you change, there is less manipulation and oppression in the world. All of life can breathe easier and relate better.

All the molecules of the ocean move in adjustment
to a drop of rain. [44]

The poem on the following page (237 words) came to me as a feeling that I estimate to have occurred in one three-hundredth of a second. It took forty-five minutes to transcribe:

[44] Samuel, John. *The Unpublished Lectures.*

Colorado Springs At Dusk

D. L. Hoefer

For the moment
the lights splashed across the foothills
could have been the markers to lost diamond mines—
reflecting light from the unfathomed Silver Mountain.
Or, they could have been great drops of dew
left by those celestial lovers of our souls
to give our lives enchantment.

For the moment,
I could have been a child again
forgetting I had left the heavens.
But the smoke, the noise, the billboards, the pavement—
they stole this moment from me
and told my soul before I even knew.
These are but extensions of the electrical, mechanical,
ideological, illogical depositories of our lives.

And I cried out!
"I don't remember how the foothills looked without the lights. Do you think we could turn out the lights?"

I only heard the echo of the Great Voice.
"If we turn out the lights, there will be chaos and crime."

Change Is Organic Unconscious And The Product Of Minute Energy Vibrations

My thoughts exploded into vapor
and I went away to a quiet place,
uncertain of who I was until my thoughts returned—
as smoke pulled from the furthest corners of a room,
back into a single puff.
    "Maybe all of our convictions are the crime
and chaos is but a reaction to them."

The Voice grew very quiet and far off.
As though it were afraid to think.
As though it were hoping I would go away.
I knew the Voice.
We had played this waiting game before,
and I felt very sad.

Chapter 9

The Seventh Principle:

You Must Become The Impartial Observer Of Yourself

The purpose of relating to your pain is not to achieve happiness but the wisdom inherent in it.

Mark Wolynn, trauma therapist, public speaker, and author, tells of a young woman who became emotionally "entangled" in the unresolved trauma of her ancestor. She came to him because she was self-harming through cutting. Wolynn asked,

"What comes to mind when you cut yourself?"

"I deserve to die," she said. But there was nothing in this person's history that would elicit such a conclusion.

Through counseling, Wolynn discovered that this woman's grandmother had killed her grandfather in a car accident while driving drunk; he determined that his client had inherited her grandmother's guilt. Her self-inflicted cuts were not unlike the wounds her grandfather suffered when he crashed through the windshield. Her guilt was not unlike the unspoken guilt of her grandmother. When this individual made the connection to the source of her trauma language — "I deserve to die"— she was able to separate from her emotional entanglement. She had been feeling shame, but it was not her shame.[45]

There is a part of you that is always watching what you do and already knowing why you do it. It is the quality of awareness that reflects and builds upon itself—allowing you to develop, mature, and become your unique self. The more impartially you observe yourself, the less biased your awareness becomes. You understand more and more of why you are as you are, who you are, and how you must be.

You inherited much from the social structure that has nothing to do with you, including morals and ethics that may reflect you but that arose from something other—a set of rules imposed by ancestors that detach you from inherent wisdom. Vague feelings, insecurities, and moods, your identification with the tribe—all the agendas that do not support you—must be separated out. This is accomplished by simply allowing, by

[45] Wolynn, Mark. "It Didn't Start with You: How Inherited Family Trauma Shapes Who We Are and How to End the Cycle." https://www.youtube.com/watch?v=YqBhAgqZGSU

impartially staying with the conflict and confusion of all the competing messages and your ongoing development. Let these independent influences buffet against themselves like turbulent wind until they coalesce into a pattern you can relate to.

You may find words to associate with the feeling, such as "I deserve to die." You might even connect the words to an event, such as, "Grandmother killed grandfather." This helps immensely in relating to your dynamic. However, it is ultimately your particular feelings themselves that orient you to your bias and hold the wisdom consciousness requires. As Wolynn said, "I believe that the contraction in a trauma is ultimately looking for its expansion [identification/understanding] and will repeat again and again [throughout succeeding generations] until that expansion happens."[46]

The purpose of relating to your pain is not to achieve happiness but the wisdom inherent in it. Allowing the pain translates into grounding, emotional depth, understanding, maturity, and meaning. Instead of "happiness," you experience neutrality, stability, spontaneity, exhilaration, and a sense of joy.

It is imperative that your understanding of: *Nothing in life —even who you have come to see yourself to be— is personal*[47] is solid, or you will never be able to observe any part of yourself. Gloom will reinforce doom. The pain of your self-image will confirm your self-hatred. Feelings of fear, shame, and blame will flare up and send you looking for that latte.

---

[46] Ibid.

[47] Leiby, John Samuel. *The Unpublished Lectures, 1978-1995.*

You Must Become The Impartial Observer Of Yourself

It is important to see your evolution as occurring independently of you. You came into being as an organic response to everything that is. This response has always been organized for optimal benefit; this organization has been, I think, in large part, a response to feelings, sensations, and the awareness that arises from them. So, when you avoid a feeling or an awareness, you argue with the organic unfolding of you.

There is you. There is your perception of what is. There are your feelings and thoughts about it all. These comprise your awareness. Mindfully give all of this to consciousness—the source from which you arise. Do nothing with these feelings and thoughts other than hold them. Remain open to any awareness that may arise about what they do, how they do it, and the source of them. Observe if you can any new feelings or understanding that may arise from your pain/body. Observe your reactions not to stop them but to mindfully bring them to awareness. As you do this, the information consciousness uses to orient and evolve you becomes less and less confused/biased; it picks and chooses, organizes, adds, and subtracts infinite possibilities. Chemistry changes, neurology, and biology changes—it speaks to you in realms beyond words.

The more you allow your observer self, the more you notice that you are doing things differently than you have in the past. For example, Jim noticed that he acted insensitively towards his co-worker Barbra. The moment Jim allows himself to be as he naturally is—without judgment—and with the knowledge that there are infinite reasons why he may be insensitive, which have nothing to do with him, the inertia of his past floods into awareness. He sees the tragedy holding him back; how he has wound his life around insensitivity to avoid feelings of isolation and loss. The moment Jim allows himself to be as he is, do you see Jim giving himself back to himself? The moment Jim notices his insensitivity—do you see sensitivity arising from within him by just acknowledging his lack of it? The moment Jim allows awareness of how he may be insensitive, the dynamic holding him becomes more visible. He feels the pain of childhood conditioning, sees how it caused him to shut down, and how the way he relates now as an adult keeps him defended and closed off.

Now, when someone challenges him, he feels overwhelming dread; the neglect and abuse of past relations arise and threaten him. Looking is painful. Experiencing himself in his pain —to the extent that he is able— allows consciousness to orient around the source of it. The more awareness Jim allows, the more courageous he becomes. He incorporates integrity and a host of attributes that exist in realms beyond words. He has more identity, more of himself to experience and express. Each moment, Jim learns more about how he has to be and what he has to do. He finds direction—his dynamic changes just by observing it.

He cannot relate to others or himself as he once did. He remembers how he once was but cannot be that person anymore. He has become more sensitive toward himself and others without even trying.

Can you see form arising out of emptiness?

Can you see being arising out of non-being?

Chapter 10

Your Intangible Self

Your feelings and sensations are the real-time nurturing that consciousness requires to bring you to a place of harmony.

If you observe our relationship from another dimension, you will see that I am in you, and you are in me—that we arise out of each other. As we converse, some beliefs are affirmed, and others discredited. As a result, you experience lightness, freedom, and spontaneity. Or you contract—become fearful and detached. Regardless of our relationship, you would sense your chemistry change.

Your feelings affect every cell of your body. Under stress, methyl groups, a modifier of gene expression, can attach to cytosine, a chemical base of DNA, creating "epigenetic" changes. Methyl attachments are typically associated with gene silencing—making it harder for a given gene to transcribe its protein.[48] Glucocorticoid receptors are reduced, increasing sensitivity to stress. Similarly, estrogen receptors

---

[48] D. Hurley (2015). "Grandma's Experiences Leave a Mark on Your Genes."

can be reduced along with the capacity for nurturing. Neural connections in the fetus may be decreased, affecting the offspring's cognition.[49] [50]

> *Szyf and others "found far more methylation [in the genes of Russian orphans'], including many that play an important role in neural communication, and brain development and function."*[51] *"People who experience racial discrimination have more methylation on the genes that affect schizophrenia, bipolar disorder, and asthma."*[52] *Szyf and Meaney, in 2008, found more methylation in the brains of suicide victims who were abused as children."*[53] [54]

Methyl attachments can be semi-permanent and passed along with the sperm or egg to offspring.[55] "For example, mice that have been taught to fear the smell of cherries when it was paired with an electric shock had children and grandchildren that also showed signs of anxiety when exposed to the odor, even though they had never "learned" [experienced] the painful association." [56] Also, "descendants of people who survived the Holocaust have different stress hormone profiles than their peers;" [57] this may predispose a

---

[49] Weaver, I. "Epigenetics in Psychology."
[50] Ibid.
[51] Hurley, D. "Grandma's Experiences Leave a Mark on Your Genes."
[52] Khazan, Olga. "Inherited Trauma Shapes Your Health."
[53] Hurley, D. "Grandma's Experiences Leave a Mark on Your Genes."
[54] Weaver, I. "Epigenetics in Psychology."
[55] Hurley, D. "Grandma's Experiences Leave a Mark on Your Genes."
[56] Khazan, Olga. "Inherited Trauma Shapes Your Health."
[57] Rodriguez, T. "Descendants of Holocaust Survivors Have Altered Stress Hormones."

succeeding generation to suffer anxiety, depression, insulin resistance, hypertension, obesity, coronary, and memory problems—even though the conditions that created the effect in the parents were never part of their children's lives.[58] [59]

> *The latest evidence, published in the Journal Science, suggests that epigenetic changes in mice are usually erased, but not always. The erasure is imperfect, and sometimes the affected genes may make it through to the next generation, setting the stage for transmission of the altered traits in descendants as well.* [60]

However, in association with other external stimuli, acetyl groups demethylase genes: Removing methyl groups from a gene is associated with gene activation—making it easier for a given gene to transcribe its protein.[61] [62] For example, pups removed from stressed mother rats and reared by nurturing ones do not have the methylation of genes affecting glucocorticoid receptors that their siblings have. These nurtured pups grow to be unstressed adults.[63]

The discovery that epigenetic changes occur in response to external stimuli supports the notion that consciousness is, as Church put it, "the organizer of matter."[64] How you

---

[58] Rodriguez, T. "Descendants of Holocaust Survivors Have Altered Stress Hormones."
[59] Khazan, Olga. "Inherited Trauma Shapes Your Health."
[60] Hurley, D. "Grandma's Experiences Leave a Mark on Your Genes."
[61] Jones, R. S. "Reversing the Irreversible."
[62] Weaver, I. "Epigenetics in Psychology."
[63] Hurley, D. "Grandma's Experiences Leave a Mark on Your Genes."
[64] Church, D. *The Genie in Your Genes, Epigenetic Medicine and the New Biology of Intention*, p. 357.

perceive yourself, your beliefs and attitudes, how you relate to your world, and how your world relates to you are all tied to how your genome is organized.[65] This thinking raises questions such as: How do you separate the way your genome is organized from a self-defeating belief and a self-defeating world? and "How do you change yourself in a consistent and optimally healthy way?"

This work's premise is that allowing the experience of your sensations and feelings as you impartially observe yourself is the precise, real-time nurturing that consciousness requires to dissolve your bias and bring you to a place of optimal expression (Chapter 14, "Feelings"). It does not matter if feeling that you are "bad," for example, arises from an irrational belief: "He or she abuses me because I'm bad." You must allow the experience of your feelings so that consciousness can orient around —get relative to— the delusion of that belief to come to understand: "He abuses me because he thinks HE is bad."

You may intellectually know that you are not bad but continue to feel the stigma of bad. Relativity removes this stigma, but you must allow the experience of your "I'm bad" belief/identity—while remaining curious, *impartial*, and observant. As you allow the information that consciousness, life, your biology, and your environment continually flood you with, without taking any of it personally —that is, without reinforcing your inherited belief with a reaction— you begin orienting to your bias, your perceptions change, and your thoughts become more affirming.

---

[65] Lipton, B. *The Biology of Belief: Unleashing the Power of Consciousness, Matter, and Miracles*

If you magnified our relationship millions of times, the lines between you and me—and everything else—would blur. You would not be able to tell where I begin and you end. You and the seat you sit on would appear to be the same. You would see that you are enmeshed with everything that is.

In this dimension, it does not matter what car I drive or where I live. I might live in a castle or under a bridge; my ethnicity and skin color are unimportant. You would experience me as energy rather than physical form. The feeling you receive from this energy would either attract or repel. Your reaction would define you as much as it would define me. You would no longer think in terms of beauty or ugliness but rather in terms of this energy dynamic that we are. You would see it expand, contract, change density, shape, and flow in relation to your proximity, thoughts, words, opinions, attitudes, and manipulations. You would see how these dimensions alter your function and the world around you, how your energy mixes with others or does not. It would be obvious why you attract or repel. It would be obvious that your perception of me directly relates to your understanding of yourself—that you arise out of me as I arise out of you. As you change, I change. Moreover, it wouldn't matter if I were a fish, insect, tree, stone, or the breath you hold in your lungs; you would see that we are interdependent entities arising out of co-creating phenomena, that we are aspects of consciousness and that we are one.

Chapter `11

Active Non-Doing

Understanding why life unfolds as it does, changes how life unfolds.

.

You are your attitude: your walk, your talk, and your manner; it is in every part of your being, your genetics, and how the elements of your body are organized. Your attitude is an exact reflection of the family, culture, and world you arose from. You are a phenomenon made up of these components, and these components are also phenomena made up of other components. Each must be as it is for things to be as they are.

Awareness of awareness allows you to observe yourself and get a sense of your position in the universe of things. The universe of things also knows your position. When you try to be different, all that is—including your own being—pushes back. You cannot change your position by disliking it any more than an element comprising your body can choose to be elsewhere. It's a paradox because the pain you are experiencing is life pressing you to be other than what you are.

But you have no way of knowing how to change yourself or what to change into—when you try, you only get more pain.

An important principle of change is that, although you may have experienced change in your life, it was not *you* who created this change. It was the awareness you allowed, the observations and connections you made, that changed you. These observations came to you because of information pressed upon you by life. This fact may seem too elementary to mention, except for all the information that life is presenting, even now, that you avoid.

Incorporating the principle that it is awareness that does the changing, removes you from the responsibility of your own evolution and allows your unique self to emerge in sync with your world. You must still earn society's educational degrees, but how you progress has everything to do with how you allow the moment-by-moment lessons life presents to incorporate. Observe yourself and your world—learn cause and effect—watch how life unfolds—understanding why life unfolds as it does, changes how life unfolds.

The notion that it is not you that creates change may not fit with your reality. Because you already know you can create any way of being that you like—and your chosen identity reinforces itself: That is, it alters perception and experience; you establish new and exciting relationships. However, when you decide how you want to be, you bypass the aliveness of becoming while not knowing what that is. You also bypass the distress of relating to your biases—the "I'm not good enough" that you react against and then reinforce in the people and experiences with which your chosen identity aligns you. The identity you affirm avoids the conflict life presents, so the underlying dynamic creating the original conflict continues to evolve. The resultant stress wears you down; it is consciousness working its way into alignment with what is.

It is the feelings themselves that provide the information life/consciousness requires to create the needed change. Allowing unpleasant feelings to penetrate your pain/body informs you on multiple tangible and intangible levels. As you stay present to your pain, you receive reflections and awareness tailored to your dynamic; seeing the value of this awareness makes the pain of "being with" more palatable, and you begin to adapt to it.

Part of this adaptation is the biological, neurological, and psychological changes that occur organically in relation to your unique feelings. Multiple levels of consciousness work in unison to bring you to the place of noticing that you have become something other. You find yourself speaking and acting in new and unexpected ways. You relate more directly to your dynamic, and your dynamic relates more directly to you. Pain is reduced or eliminated. This new you is never what you expect it to be. However, it always expresses greater connection, identity, stability, and the stillness required to observe your dynamic in greater depth.

Seeing the intricacy of this dynamic that is you is a requirement of understanding. You have come to understand many things, and you have understood these things to the degree that you were able to observe.

To observe, you must be still. You cannot understand the ripples in a pond that you are reacting against. Active non-doing speaks to the attentive stillness required to be in the pond while observing your influence upon it—and its influence upon you.

The ripples in the pond have nothing to do with the pond itself. Things being as they are—the life forms, the wind, the rain, the pull of the moon, the spin of the earth—create the ripples in the pond. Understanding arises from the awareness that allows everything to be as it is: the president, the Congress, the social structure, and yourself—allowing awareness of the why of the why of your predicament repositions you.

You cannot exist in the universe with an expanded awareness and remain in the same position you were in before receiving this awareness. The why of the why affects you whether you are aware of it or not, whether you argue with it or not. However, the less relative you are to cause and effect, the more troublesome that effect can be. As you allow awareness, you reposition in the most constructive way: Everything is more understandable; you see that everything, including you, is exactly as it should be; this "should be" is precisely related to awareness. Understanding changes your walk-through life, your evolutionary trajectory, and your maturity. It feeds back upon itself and builds multi-dimensionally in ways that you could never foretell.

Chapter 12

Being You

How do you reconfigure yourself
when every part of you is identified with every other part
and with the dynamic out of which they arise?

This essence that is you, cannot be defined. You can relate to it but never put it into words. You share as best you can your thoughts and feelings, your ways of connecting with others, and your sense of humor, but you cannot share your essence with anyone. This isn't noted to create sadness but rather to relate to at least one aspect of the sadness you have —your aloneness. It has to be this way, because you are unique. There is no one like you, now, nor will there ever be anyone like you again.

If you do not learn to relate to your aloneness, the maturity to be who you are will never grow in you. So, an aspect of being a person is being in some ways alone, and an aspect of being alone is being autonomous: acting independently of others to whatever degree is required for you to be you. You can only be yourself by yourself; if you go against yourself by becoming enmeshed in the methodologies and definitions of others, you begin to fragment. Fragmented is what you become in the social structure, in the environment where everyone is required to think and act like everyone else. How do you separate out and allow this essence that you are to be?

I began to get a sense of who I am and what I am about by acknowledging what I was not: I was not the self-image that I didn't like, nor was I the self-image that I projected, hoping it would someday be the real me. I was not my history, education, career, or conditioning. Nor was I all the things I did to be accepted and loved, to feel good about myself. I was not the unconscious reaction I apologized for and tried to suppress. I was not good, nor was I bad. I was not the stigma I identified with, nor was I what I had been taught to think and believe. I was not even my intelligence, interests, or discoveries.

Everything I used to define myself and set myself apart, placed me within a matrix of non-being, of living out a programmed existence. My life became a ritual, choreographed before my birth, that had nothing to do with who I am. My house, my career, my religion, my education, my self-image—all were amalgamations of fears, superstitions, and attitudes that had been passed down. These provided social position and placed me within a family, tribe, and nation. I had the thought, but it was not my thought.

Letting go of what you are not, may feel like going from something to nothing: it may feel empty and confusing—a loss of traction. You experience all of the unresolved conflicts within and around you that you were previously avoiding. As you allow identification with what you are not to fall away, as you allow what is to coalesce, your flickering light begins to shine. *Truth is a fragile energy, like the flame of a candle carried through a breezeway —so easily blown out.*[66] Being what you are not—being untrue—turns this fragile energy into smoke.

You must discover what is true for you and align with it in everything you do; this is not a thinking process, so much as a feeling process. You sense where you need to be and not be, what you need to do to stay connected to this fragile energy that is you. As the sense of your essence becomes more distinct, what you can and cannot do becomes more defined. However, you will never know this completely, because the parameters from which you arise are constantly changing. Discover what clouds this delicate essence and what lets it shine.

Your truths arise from the sensations and feelings of preverbal awareness; they expand, contract, coalesce, and form anew in every moment. Your truth is the awareness needed to carry your essence through the corridors of life without extinguishing it. In certain realms, you hold it as a naked flame; in others, you contain it in a lamp. In yet others, you shield it so no light shines. Do not share your truth with anyone who will not receive it. When you are cut off, minimized, redirected, or disregarded, consciousness is injured.

Relate to those who will allow and even support this or that part of your reality, so that you can see it, reflect, and try

---

[66] Leiby, John Samuel. *The Unpublished Lectures, 1978-1995.*

different perspectives. You must "be with" your uniqueness instead of denying, analyzing, and diagnosing it. Stop seeking more comfortable ways of being with what you do not like about yourself. You must allow what you are to coalesce into a form you can relate to. Then, as you relate to your evolving form, this uniqueness that is you finds ways to express itself.

The shape of your essence is unlike any other and determines your uniqueness. It is how energy moves through you and how sensations coalesce into feelings, thoughts, perceptions, and ways of being. Think of the shapes of clouds: some are luminous plumes of down, others stream at high altitudes as aerosol crystals of ice. Yet others are dark and dense, blotting the sun, exploding without warning in thunder, lightning, and rain.

The shape of clouds may seem like an odd analogy of your essence, but think of how you come and go like a cloud in an otherwise transparent sky. Think of how parts of you seem distinct and build upon each other, while other parts become diffuse and vague; how thoughts come easily at times, or not. Think of what you have been and what you have become and how what you are, changes from day to day. Think of all the phenomena that create these effects. It is not the cloud that creates these effects; instead, these effects arise out of the phenomena that create the cloud. This is not an attempt to excuse what you have become, but to understand the source of it, and by understanding, change the phenomena out of which you arise. Everything in the universe is much like everything else. We are made of stardust and subject to the same laws of physics.

You must allow the experience of your reality in every way you can to add awareness to the dynamic that this "source" must navigate so that it/you can evolve. Most of what you feel you cannot verbalize; most of what you are cannot be defined. However, being with what is allows the conflicts and the vagaries of life to coalesce into a form you can relate to with ever-increasing clarity.

The most crucial aspect of coalescence is actively looking for, allowing, and observing your fears, conflicts, reactions, and inconsistencies; these point to the biases that reinforce themselves, convolute energy, and create turbulence. Biases block the integration of you with you. There are just a few, but they keep energy confused and stagnant. Though there are just a few biases, the nuances of poor self-esteem, anger, and self-judgment seem endless. The "I'm not good enough" that crops up in different ways, like shoots from a weed you thought you cut down. It takes patience and courage. Feelings of inferiority can never resolve themselves when you keep reinforcing them with a reaction.

If the shape of your essence were that of a cloud, how would you relate to it? Like me, you may have been given everything as a child except intimacy and connection. As a result, you may have difficulty connecting meaningfully with yourself and your world. The question is, how would you change that? How would you know what bonding looks like in you? You may see parents interacting with their children in ways that you never experienced, but how can you retrofit your perceptions into a matrix of experience denied to you from birth? How would you know to combine this part with that without fragmenting yourself? How do you reconfigure yourself when every part of you is identified with every other part and with the dynamic out of which they arise?

Consciousness knows the meaning of your shape
—you do not.

The courage to be me arises from allowing/experiencing my painful feelings when I behave in ways I disapprove of. Feelings add awareness to my pain/body and show consciousness, where I need maturity and connection. Each time I notice that I am distracted from myself, each time I notice how I sabotage myself, I move a millisecond closer to being more with myself. The more I am with myself, the more present I become, and the more real-time information I incorporate, showing consciousness how and where I need mending.

Staying with your truth evolves into your unique set of morals, ethics you cannot go against without going against your *self*. As you hold your truths, you sense yourself coming into and going out of accord. If you are true, your world becomes less conflicted. If you are untrue, your world becomes more conflicted. If you cannot tell if your world is more or less conflicted, it is best to simply be with the complexity of your feelings; this allows the discordant influences to coalesce until you know within yourself how you must be and what you must do.

Everything you incorporate also becomes part of the world around you, feeds back, and builds upon itself; this is the reality of your value, which you cannot appreciate when you are enmeshed in the social structure. Detached from your *self*, you reinforce the social dogmas that spawn trite goals and intentions, such as the idea that you must sacrifice yourself for the greater good. To the extent that you incorporate these beliefs, you overlook your essence and discredit the value of *being*.

Instead, you must recognize that you are the most important person on the planet. On Spaceship Earth, as on a malfunctioning aircraft, you must stabilize yourself before assisting those floundering around you. If everyone is preoccupied with doing what they believe will be approved, who is left to see their value apart from good works? Who is left to improvise? Who is left to *be*?

Chapter 13

Phenomena

With this attitude, you get this deed,
and with this deed, you get that outcome
—now or in one hundred years.

Practitioners often use Universal Laws to acquire what they want in life. However, pursuing what you want can distract you from what you must learn from your predicament: That is, rather than counteracting your attitude with love, joy, and gratitude to create a better experience, understand why these feelings are not already arising from within you of their own accord. Nevertheless, the conceptual framework provided by these laws helps us relate to the phenomena of life. Among these Laws are:

The Law of Action: *Your thoughts, feelings, and deeds create direction.*

The Law of Attraction: *Like attracts like. Whatever you receive is directly related to your thoughts and deeds.*

The Law of Polarity: *Everything has a positive and a negative aspect. Without shadows, there is no contrast or perception.*

The Law of Oneness: *Whatever you think or do affects you and the dynamic out of which you arise.*

The Law of Vibration: *Everything vibrates at a unique frequency; higher vibrations = positive beliefs, emotions, and experiences.*

The Law of Relativity: *Everything in the universe arises out of and receives its form and meaning from everything else.*[67]

The Law of Gender: *Your potential is greatest when there is a balance between the masculine and feminine.*

The Law of Cause and Effect: *Your experience directly relates to your thoughts, feelings, attitudes, deeds,*[68] *and perceptions.*

---

[67] Purify Mind, "Form and Emptiness."
[68] Self-Made Ladies, 12 Universal Laws for Manifestation. https://selfmadeladies.com/universal-laws/#universallaw6

If you think about it, though, there is a law created by the combination of each of the various laws, such as how a given amount of polarity affects action, how a given amount of action affects attraction, and how a given amount of attraction affects the gender balance, etc. Then, there is the degree to which a combination of laws uniquely contributes to a given phenomenon, like polarity, attraction, or action. In short, the laws (influences) we interact with at any moment are infinite and unnamable.

Relating to infinite phenomena by attending to a few laws is the definition of a bias. It is impossible to walk this tightrope we call life from a biased perspective. There is too much information and too many dynamics to attend to. When you try to simplify what is not simple, when you try to separate what cannot be separated, you bias biology, well-being, and evolution.

It is more meaningful to relate to unnamable and evolving phenomena than it is to relate to a set of memorized laws. Tolle said, "God is infinite by our definition. But we do not relate to infinity; we relate to God, thereby reducing the infinite invisible to a finite entity."[69] You can know phenomena even though you cannot put them into words. You can relate to phenomena by immersing yourself in the associated feelings and unnamable sensations. You can marvel at the interplay of cause and effect, and you can learn what you can do and what you cannot do while still maintaining integrity. What you receive from life is never what you think it is, and never what you were looking for:

---

[69] Tolle, E. "Practicing the Power of Now," p. 9.

Your "I'm unlovable" belief conflicts with the intimacy you enjoy and perverts your relationship.

Focusing on a formula for getting what you want overlooks the phenomena creating your need. Your intention counteracts the solution life is bringing. You are on the wrong track. You have a train wreck and all the cars you were pulling crash into you one by one. The train wreck shows the formula you have been unwittingly operating by. If you are open to it, it will also show you the fear, the "I'm not good enough" that put you on the wrong track, and the "I'm not good enough" that caused you to mistrust your gut. Now, your gut does not trust you. Observe yourself. Look for what you do and why you do it, what you are and what you are not—without reacting by taking what you have become personally; this orients you to life, and life on its own knows how to thrive.

Out of presence emerges the geometry of cause and effect. You begin to appreciate the interwoven, multi-layered tapestry of influence, of being and non-being, doing and non-doing, stretching back over time. "These influences are primed like time bombs set to trigger at the culmination of events—when you hear something, meet someone, or even attain a certain age."[70] With this attitude, you get this deed, and with this deed, you get that outcome—now or in one hundred years. Whatever nurtures or destroys builds upon

[70] Leiby, John Samuel. *The Unpublished Lectures, 1978-1995*

itself and continues forever. You create it with the wave of your hand. This new thing—this new way of being, now—adds to it all. It is an energy, a life-form all its own, looking for relationship. There is no shame in it. Whatever comes into being teaches wisdom. Life only cares about wisdom.

It can be as simple as returning a pair of pants and then breaking a bottle of wine as you leave the store. "Coincidence!" you say. But coincidence happens all the time. It arises from your thoughts, your fears, and deeds.

This geometry is within you, but it also surrounds you. The cost you inflict is inflicted upon you. The assumptions you make of others are made of you. Your experience is the reflection of every attitude, every act—what you have done and what was done before you came into being. All these influences are within and without, working for and against each other for resolve. Energy working against energy resolves itself.

What is needed is the intention to understand. Understanding changes everything; it orients, coalesces, and nurtures what was extraneous and unwanted—it unifies and makes whole. The awareness, the understanding, and the wisdom come as you become still—as you observe how energy resolves itself.

Chapter 14

Feelings

Most of what you are exists in the preverbal realm.

Jen believed that she was unlovable and found imperfection in everything she did. She suppressed her feelings to avoid the pain. With her feelings blunted, she didn't know what she was about: She could not trust herself. She could not find direction. She felt cut off. Feeling cut off, she did not express herself well and discounted her wisdom. She couldn't grow. She disliked herself and entered relationships based on momentary desires and wishful thinking. In this trajectory, she was easily manipulated and exploited. Every interaction reinforced the cycle of shutting down. She felt defenseless, and logic didn't work. Her biases created blind spots that allowed her peers to disregard her, in the same way she had been disregarded as a child. She looked for relief in isolation, drugs, and endless distractions.

All thoughts and awareness originate as sensations that coalesce into feelings, which you later interpret as perceptions, beliefs, and your identity. A thought, then, is a coalesced feeling. Because of this, feelings can trigger thoughts, and thoughts can trigger feelings. For example, Jen told herself she was unlovable because she felt unlovable. Thoughts are abstractions of feelings. Therefore, while finding ways to convince herself that she was not unlovable, counteracted her feeling of being unlovable, it did nothing to dissolve her core belief that she *was* unlovable.

This is because the word "unlovable" is a generalized label Jen used to describe a complex of feelings that were unique to her. Until she related directly to this "feeling complex," Jen's sense of being "unlovable" would be triggered again and again. Allowing/grieving the nuances of her belief/identity with all its confused, hurt, and lonely consequences—made available the precise information consciousness needed to orient Jen to her *self.*

No one else has your unique complex of feelings/sensations associated with "unlovable/insufficient;" this "feeling complex" contains the only information that can speak to your particular "insufficient" identity/belief/conditioning; this communication occurs by and large on the preverbal—biological/genetic level, so trying to analyze it is crazy-making. Your feelings and beliefs arise from each other; metaphysically, they are one and the same. As you allow the experience of your unique complex of feelings without reacting —that is, remaining impartial—their underlying beliefs and conditioning also stop being reinforced and, as a result, begin to dissolve. As you stop reacting to one part of your identity, you stop reinforcing the other; without the belief/conditioning, you cannot experience the feeling; this also works in reverse—without the feeling, historical beliefs and conditioning cannot trigger you (Chapter 26, "The Three-Legged-Stool").

Most of what we are exists in the preverbal realm. For example, over half of our body's cells aren't human. They are microbes composed of bacteria, bacteriophages, prokaryotes, viruses, and fungi that live primarily in our gut but also on the surface of our skin, in our blood, and within every cell. They break food down into absorbable nutrients and create vitamins like B12, biotin, and folic acid; they assist with gene transcription, methylation, and acetylation (Chapter 10, Your "Intangible Self"), gene splicing, cell division, and creating our immune response. They communicate with our nervous system, and our nervous system communicates with them using neurotransmitters, their precursors, and other hormones:

> *Metabolites (e.g., short-chain fatty acids, neurotransmitters [glutamate, GABA, serotonin, and dopamine] [19,29,32]., and their precursors) [31,32,33] produced by bacteria affect the levels of related metabolites in the brain via the blood circulation, thus regulating brain functions and cognition [10,11,12]. [In addition], some gut bacteria can signal via their metabolites to regulate the synthesis and release of neurotransmitters by intestinal enteroendocrine cells, which can act locally on the enteral nervous system or transmit fast signals to the brain via the vagus nerve*

[13,30,31].[71] [Conversely], binding sites for enteric neurotransmitters produced by the host are present on bacteria and can influence the function of components of the microbiota [67]..[72] Changes in the abundance of neurotransmitters like serotonin may signal changes that bacteria need to respond to, such as immune activity or flow through the gut lumen. In this way, neurotransmitters may not only represent a means of neuron–neuron communication, but also a way for hosts to communicate with their microbiota. [73]

---

[71] Chen, Yijing [1] Xu, Jinying [1,2] and Chen, Yu.[1] (2021). Francavilla, Ruggiero, Academic Editor, *Regulation of neurotransmitters by the Gut Microbiota and Effects on Cognition in Neurological Disorders, Nutrients*, The National Library of Medicine, Jun 19. Regulation of Neurotransmitters by the Gut Microbiota and Effects on Cognition in Neurological Disorders - PMC (nih.gov)

[72] Gastroenterol,· Ann (2015). "The gut-brain axis: interactions between enteric microbiota, central and enteric nervous systems," *Annals of Gastroenterology*, Apr-Jun. From: https://www.ncbi.nlm.nih.gov/pmc/articles/PMC4367209/

[73] Lynch, Jonathan B., Hsiao, Elaine Y. (2023). "Toward understanding links between the microbiome and neurotransmitters," Annals of the New York Academy of Sciences,_: 05 April 2023: https://nyaspubs.onlinelibrary.wiley.com/doi/10.1111/nyas.14993

Collectively, they multiply the coding potential of our own 20,500 [74] genome by 100 (estimated).[75] Physiology forms the foundation for perception, but all of its complexity occurs without a single self-aware thought.

When these same microbes are stressed by environmental cues: toxins, pathogens, antibiotics, diet, and emotional turmoil,[76] they can turn against the host—interfering with gene transcription, blocking the immune response, and creating inflammation. Numerous diseases and conditions are implicated with microbial imbalances (dysbiosis): inflammatory bowel disease, asthma, diabetes, several cancers, periodontitis (gum disease), cardiovascular disease,

---

[74] Proal, Amy D, Lindseth, Inge A and Trevor G Marshall (2007). "Microbe-microge and host-microbe interactions drive microbiome dysbiosis and inflammatory processes," *Pub Med,* Jan 2. https://pubmed.ncbi.nlm.nih.gov/28245427/

[75] Nichols, Robert G. and Davenport, Emily R. (2020). The relationship between the gut microbiome and host gene expression: a review, *The National Institute of Health,* Nov 22. The relationship between the gut microbiome and host gene expression: a review - PMC (nih.gov)

[76] Gastroenterol, Ann, Carabotti, Marilia, Scirocco, Annunziata, Maselli, Maria Antonietta and Seven, Carola (2015). The gut-brain axis: interactions between enteric microbiota, central and enteric nervous systems, Annals of Gastroenterology, Apr-Jun. https://www.ncbi.nlm.nih.gov/pmc/articles/PMC4367209/

metabolism (low energy), Parkinson's, anxiety, depression, autism, obesity, and psoriatic and rheumatoid arthritis. [77] [78]

This work's premise is that, by impartially allowing your feelings to penetrate mind/body, you give consciousness the precise information needed to orient around the tangible and intangible aspects of being. I'm not saying that this is the total solution, but the science of epigenetics suggests that our unique "feeling complex" relates to every protein in our bodies. These proteins, in turn, influence our health or disease. As you acknowledge (stay with) your conflict/fear, its underlying influence is incrementally discredited/dissolved. The overpowering bully of your childhood loses influence. You stop running, dodging, and hiding; you receive awareness you could not receive under any other circumstance and become increasingly relative.

Feelings connect you to your dynamic in real-time. Allowing your irrational feelings connects you to your irrational beliefs. Mindfully allowing the painful feeling of "I'm unlovable" took Jen to the source of her belief: How her reactions against discrediting now as an adult reinforced the discrediting she received as a child. Even when Jen could not

---

[77] Kinross, James M, Darzi, Ara W., Nicholson, Jeremy K. (2011). Gut microbiome-host interactions in health and disease, *Genome Medicine,* 4 March.
https://genomemedicine.biomedcentral.com/articles/10.1186/gm228

[78] Zhang, Shujun, Xu, Quin Li, Xiaotao, Chen, Jingyao, Liu, Siyu, Zhao, Wenming , Cai, Huanhuan, Zhu, Jiajia, Yu, Yonggiang (2019). Crosstalk Between the Gut Microbiota and the Brain: An Update on Neuroimaging Findings. *Frontiers in Neurology,* 13 August.
https://www.frontiersin.org/articles/10.3389/fneur.2019.00883/full

find the source or the words to describe her beliefs or the dynamic they arose from, staying with the pain of her feelings worked to unravel her conditioning. Irrational feelings, experienced *impartially,* dissolve their underlying irrational belief.

Jen's identity evolved out of her infantile emotive self. Before she was born, she absorbed her mother's attitude and the tension between her parents. Her birth was not part of their plan—they even told her so. After her birth, as she developed and became cognitive, she interpreted her inherited feeling as "I'm unlovable." She tried in a thousand ways, as any child would, to be close to parents who were seemingly incapable of accepting her. Then, as an adult, whenever someone wanted to be close to her, her "I'm unlovable" got triggered. The more she tried to counter "unlovable," the more intensely she feared rejection. The more she feared rejection, the more she sabotaged her relationships. The more she sabotaged, the more she demonstrated to herself and others that she was unlovable. Everything she did to prove she was not unlovable reinforced her belief that she was.

We identify early on with the irrational beliefs of our parents because children do not develop logical thinking until the age of twelve.[79] It is impossible to have a rational thought before you have a rational mind. We absorb our parent's self-image because we incorporate the feeling of being "insufficient," for example before we "recognize the difference between [ourselves] and [our] environment." A

---

[79] Stanford Children's Health/Lucile Packard Children's Hospital, "Cognitive Development in the Teen Years." Cognitive Development in Adolescence - Stanford Medicine Children's Health

child's sense of physical boundaries develops around two months of age.[80] Around age twelve, as our minds become increasingly rational, we come into conflict with our inherited identity.

Using logic to counteract an irrational belief is irrational because whatever logic you use reinforces the belief you are attempting to counteract. For example, Jen would not be working to be acceptable if she didn't already believe she was unacceptable. In this way, logic becomes convoluted, working against itself, creating thoughts tied to feelings, triggering troublesome beliefs and conditioned reactions. Fear ignited fear, and Jen either became controlled and guarded, losing spontaneity and self-expression, or she experienced a runaway mind. This phenomenon manifests as panic attacks, anxiety, depression, isolation, mood swings, and the need for distraction. Allowing awareness of her reactions created the space Jen needed for focus.

Jen knew her self-image wasn't true, so she initially worked to counteract it, instead of finding relativity to it; that is, impartially identifying the influences that shaped her. However, noticing how she reacted permitted Jen to identify the fear (unique feeling) she was reacting against and gradually allowed her to face it. Allowing awareness of how she had shut down her feelings worked to open her to the experience of them. Allowing the awareness that she did not

---

[80] Krisch, J. A. "The Five Stages Of Self-Awareness Explain When Babies Recognize Themselves In The Mirror." The 5 Stages Of Self-Awareness Explain What Babies See In The Mirror

want to see herself for who and what she had become supported the development of whatever qualities that were needed to become self-observant.

Allowing the feeling of being "unlovable" for as long as it lasted while remaining impartial and curious, connected Jen to her belief/identity and the source of it. As she experienced her identity and reflected on how she came by it, how her efforts to oppose it reinforced it, and how the dynamic she found herself in supported it, she began to separate from it; that is, she noticed the feeling was still triggering her on occasion, but that she was no longer identifying with the feeling. The less she identified with unlovable/insufficient, the less she worked to control how others perceived her. The less she controlled, the less she reinforced "unlovable" and all the related feelings and social conditioning connected to it. In the process, she discovered her blind spots and learned about her strengths, weaknesses, and injuries—where she needed growth and repair.

Allowing awareness, repositioned her. It is like kung fu: as you orient to an attack, you nullify it. As Jen separated out, her inherited identity triggered her less and less, gradually ceasing to affect her at all. It became irrelevant. She could recall believing she was unlovable but couldn't identify with that feeling anymore.

Chapter 15

Grief

The value of life is you.

When my father died, I grieved the bond that had never happened. The feelings and sensations showed me how I was wounded: the self-judgment, aloofness, isolation, and the terrible inferiority I had inherited. Observing how I cut myself off from those offering connections was a step in allowing surrogate parents and, to some extent, re-parenting myself.

There is great wisdom inherent in your losses. They are life's precious gift—exposing the ongoing effect of trauma inherited from those who came before. Grieving your loss and allowing into awareness the sorrow, regret, and torment of it—the memories, the circumstances, and tangential images—gives back what was missing in you and your dynamic when the loss occurred. Moreover, doing so requires you to orient, coalesce, and define—with ever more clarity—what and who you are. As you become more defined, everything around you becomes more defined.

Feelings are exhaustible. They only have a given amount of energy, so they can not last forever. You already know this. You may have distracted yourself from depression by going to the movies. You may have slept in and used sex, drugs, and alcohol to get past feelings of frustration, anger, isolation, and shame; these are all unfortunate conclusions to your knowing that feelings cannot last forever.

You must be careful here because without a conscious decision to do so (e.g., "I need a break from self-discovery.") distractions can become additionally conditioned ways of coping that consciousness/life must now unravel. When you evade the pain of a loss, you evade the wisdom inherent in it and perpetuate unresolved dynamics that require another expenditure of equal or greater value by you or someone else (Wolyn, Chapter 9).

Receiving what was missing—filling in the vacant spaces hollowed out before your birth—is like graduating from school. The pain, anguish, and cost all make up the tuition required for you to become you. Stay with your losses; refer to them time and again. Each review grounds and matures you, giving back more of what you didn't appreciate, more of what contributed to your unique dynamic. It repositions you. The vacuum of your loss is filled with meaning and depth that could not be acquired in any other way. Your grief is countered with gratitude.

Chapter 16

Shame

You have a responsibility to be truthful,
to apologize and make amends,
but not to take what you have become personally.

Dr. Ofri tells of a near-fatal mistake she made during her second-year residency while treating a patient in a diabetic coma. When confronted by a senior assistant, "humiliation set in." She said: *I could almost feel myself dying away on the spot. In fact, for many minutes, that seemed preferable. I wanted to evaporate, to disappear, to expire from that horrific moment of shame.* Years later, Dr. Ofri re-connected with this senior assistant at a conference. As they casually conversed, "the shame of [her] error" came to mind "and the resultant loss of self-esteem [that] would not release their grip."[81]

It is an interesting phenomenon, don't you think, that Dr. Ofri experienced personal disintegration over an action she had

[81] Lyons, Barry, Gibson, Matthew, Dolezal, Luna (2018). *Stories of Shame, The Lancet,* April 21. https://www.thelancet.com/journals/lancet/article/PIIS0140-6736%2818%2930897-3/fulltext

no way of knowing was an error before she took it? We, humans, learned early on that we could get others to behave in ways we wanted by stigmatizing them—causing them to feel bad about themselves. Virtually every authority figure uses it: parents, schools, religions, courts, and governments. As of this notice, China posts images to shame jaywalkers—and it works![82]

The problem, though, is that to use shame against others, we have to believe in it ourselves. As author Krista Thomason writes, "Shame is morally valuable because it is indicative of moral maturity." [83] Many people believe that without shame, there would be no moral motive; as a result, they think better of themselves for their ability to experience it. As she continues, "I recognize the standing of others—moral sensitivities that shameless individuals lack." [84]

I doubt that without the childhood influences (trauma) that incorporated irrational identities, Dr. Ofri would have experienced shame; instead, she would have merely expressed regret and then channeled her energies toward correcting her mistake. It would have been impossible for her to associate an error with "I'm insufficient/unworthy" (shame) if she hadn't been conditioned to do so. That is, it is impossible to fire a gun without first installing a bullet.

Shame is a driver; it presses us to achieve things we might not otherwise have achieved—like becoming a doctor. But then, without that driver, would we have become something more in line with who we naturally are? It takes a lot of "doing" (energy)

---

[82] China shames jaywalkers through facial recognition, *Phys.Org,* June 20, 2017: https://phys.org/news/2017-06-china-shames-jaywalkers-facial-recognition.html

[83] Thomason, Krista. *Naked: The Dark Side of Shame and Moral Life*

[84] Ibid.

to keep our shame shadow at bay. When my "I'm defective belief" (Chapter 26, "The Three-Legged-Stool") was resolved, I gained what felt like 25% more mental capacity.

The problem with these "I'm bad" identities (always inflicted by degrees of abuse) is that they have a way of creating problems many times worse than they were meant to solve; shame is linked to depression, suicide,[85] violence, murder,[86] and mass shootings.[87]

Shame and the effects of shame are so intertwined that it is difficult to separate the "I'm bad" identity of a parent from the insensitivity experienced by their children: Callousness is an emotional defense against abuse, and the trauma of insensitivity is passed down unconsciously through the generations. I recall feeling disappeared when my father read the newspaper by holding it in front of his face. You may not remember all the subtle and overt ways that you were shamed as a child—for being clumsy before you developed manual dexterity, for breaking things before you learned cause and effect, for not understanding before you developed logical thinking, and for simply existing; you may have laughingly been called "butterfingers," but the experience was devastating. Now, whenever you feel the

---

[85] Weingarden, Hilary, Reinshaw, Keith D., Wilhelm, Sabine, Tangney, June P., DiMauro, Jennifer (2017). *Anxiety and Shame as Risk Factors for Depression, Duicidality, and Functional Impairment in Body Dysmorphic Disorder and Obsessive Compulsive Disorder,* National Library of Medicine, PMC Nov 1: https://www.ncbi.nlm.nih.gov/pmc/articles/PMC5026856/

[86] Gillian, James (2003). *Shame, Guilt, and Violence, 70(*4). John Hopkins University Press. https://www.jstor.org/stable/40971965

[87] Warner, Melanie (2022). "Two Professors Found What Creates a Mass Shooter: Will Politicians Pay Attention?" *Politico Magazine,* 05/27. https://www.politico.com/news/magazine/2022/05/27/stopping-mass-shooters-q-a-00035762

humiliation of a rebuke or mistake, your "I'm not good enough" gets triggered.

Relate to shame, not by fighting against it, but by simply noticing how you are caught in it and remaining curious. Observe yourself in this spectacle of reproach, how reactions to your mistakes are used by yourself and others to reinforce your "I'm bad" identity, how feelings of shame precipitate shameful deeds—how attempts to explain only add to your humiliation.

Try to get a sense of the unique quality of your shame—the indifference, the betrayal, all the triggers of your conditioning and experience. If it is more than you can let in, in the moment, notice that. Just noticing what you cannot give to awareness works to build in you whatever qualities are needed to observe yourself and walk with dignity. As you allow the experience of your most dreadful feelings without taking any of them personally, the underlying beliefs/conditioning creating shame and self-loathing stop being reinforced and begin to dissolve (Chapter 14, "Feelings"); this occurs even if you cannot fully identify what those beliefs and conditioning are.

In the spirit of the old Mission Impossible line, "Your mission, should you choose to accept it," is to be the first in your family line to identify this self-defeating dynamic, stop reacting to it, and let it fade into oblivion. By allowing shame to unfold as it will, you see the source of it and that it has nothing to do with who you are. You have a responsibility to be truthful, to apologize, and make amends, but not to take what you have become personally.

Chapter 17

Depression

As you course-correct in your own life,
you might reasonably feel for a time,
that you are moving in the wrong emotional direction.[88]

Sometime during my twenty-first year, I drove my little red Honda 160 motorcycle to a very straight stretch of lonely desert road in the Phoenix area of Arizona. I paused there for a moment, struck by the surreality of the place—the random symmetry of Mesquite, Saguaro, and deer grass—and the stillness of it. Easy breezes caressed and nudged me, and there was my wonderment at the freedom of sparrows calling out and flitting from branch to branch; this contrasted starkly with the oppressive cacophony of my mind and spirit. It would have been well for me to spend the day in the shade of an ironwood relating to the harmony that engulfed me. But there was a question I needed to know the answer to, so I pulled back the throttle and held it till I stopped accelerating, and the needle danced about the eighty-mph mark, closed my eyes, and counted to ten. I had visions of ramming the back of a

[88] Leiby, John Samuel. *The Unpublished Lectures,* 1978-1995.

truck, veering off the road, or colliding with an oncoming car, but when I opened my eyes, there was only the roar of the motor, the warm wind slapping my pant legs, and the pavement flying beneath my feet; "I guess—I'm not supposed to die."

A caveat:

When I decided to embrace my depression, although doing so felt like black on black, I noticed that accidents reduced, and I stopped being suicidal.

Chögyam Trungpa exiled Tibetan meditation master and founder of Naropa University in Boulder, Colorado,[89] shared the ancient Buddhist teaching with his student, W. T., who, in turn, shared it with me: "Embrace your depression." The wisdom of it resonated with every molecule of my body: "If depression is an aspect of who I am, and I evade depression, I evade myself. No wonder I'm depressed!"

My experience with embracing severe depression felt like throwing myself into a turbulent river and letting the current carry me haplessly, topsy-turvy, hither and yon—where it will. I had quit fighting/arguing against my inherited identity and was now allowing my sensations and feelings to expose the truth of myself; it felt like diving to the bottom of the ocean. Each observation took me deeper, revealing aspects I didn't like; it felt like drowning—but I would not drown. For forty-nine years, my beliefs had reinforced my identity, and my identity had reinforced my beliefs. Now, I could only

---

[89] https://en.wikipedia.org/wiki/Ch%C3%B6gyam_Trungpa

watch without interfering with what I observed: I knew that if I tried to counteract (react against) the negative aspects of my self-image, I would only reinforce them.

I felt worthless and asked the universe while remaining curious, where, with this terrible cloud over my head, could I find the maturity to walk through life? I thought that by identifying with the most loathsome creature, I could at least *be*. A worm, at least, has no aversion toward itself. So, I decided to become the worm. I lay on my back on the floor of my room, arms, and legs spread-eagled —the most vulnerable position I could find— to let the most fearsome versions of myself come to mind, holding with every breath the pain of my existence. As I exhaled, I cried to the universe, "If you think that version of me was pathetic, what about this one." And I conjured something even more despicable for my next breath.

Enhanced versions of my contemptibility made traditional ones seem bland. Manufacturing personal insults —while remaining impartial— made a mockery of the evasion I had engaged in throughout life. This exercise gave relativity: I discovered that I was despicable to this degree but not to that degree, this confused but not that. It gave position along a trajectory that allowed me to observe my progress over time. It gave hope.

I didn't know it at the time, but impartially observing myself as I experienced my most dreadful feelings worked to discredit the beliefs underlying my inherited self-image. Feelings and beliefs arise from each other. By not reacting to mitigate either —allowing each to be as they were—even exploring the possibility that I had identified with more negativity than was true— neither feeling nor belief was reinforced. Not being reinforced, they could not be sustained: Without the belief, the feeling could not exist; without the feeling, the belief could not exist.

I could only observe myself because I had become crystalline with the idea that I am a phenomenon, the product of a dynamic: *Nothing in life —even who I have come to see myself to be— is personal.*[90] I had to look at what I considered to be my negative traits in a constructive way—to see mistakes, immaturity, and dysfunction as sources of good information.

Throughout this exercise, there were moments I feared I might lose my mind, so I would get up off the floor and make a cup of tea. It seemed masochistic because, although every cell of my body was on fire, the pain conjured images of my life and awareness of the dynamics entrapping me that were both ironic and profound. Just seeing the relationship of cause and effect had such an exquisite aspect that I found a part of myself looking forward to these episodes of delving within.

The torture ended, but not because I ran from it. I allowed it to teach me for as long as it lasted. I awoke one morning after three months of terrible sadness, fear, and agony—more pain than I thought a body could hold—to find my lifelong depression was essentially gone. I felt more integrated than ever before. Periods of sadness came and went, but never to the intensity that I had experienced in my previous life. My conflicted self seemed to have consumed itself.

---

[90] Leiby, John Samuel. *The Unpublished Lectures, 1978-1995.*

For the next fifteen years, I quit reading books, going to therapy, or attending classes for self-discovery. I realized that only I could sort out the nuances of me. This acknowledgment contained the understanding that it wasn't me that was sorting me out; it was the incremental changes that came from allowing the particular feelings, the courage, and integrity to see and be with what I am—the interplay of every form of awareness I was able to allow—that sorted me out.

Sometimes, a perception created a new way of being. Other times, it was the gradual disbelieving that comes from allowing what is, while impartially observing myself being whatever I was, with the question, "Isn't that interesting?" As my beliefs about myself changed, I changed and became something other. I noticed I walked differently and paid more attention to how I dressed. I related to others differently, and others related differently to me. Dynamics changed. Finances improved.

It helps to be open to all the ways you may be injured. When you go to the hospital with a complaint, the staff examines you thoroughly; they do not look only at the area troubling you. A specific ailment may arise from multiple sources. As you explore your pain, it appears to intensify; your body can only experience so much of it. You cannot sink below your own depths, but as you attend to your pain, the denial of your injury falls away, and you feel the real intensity of your loss; this is the requirement of separating from (becoming relative to) inherited trauma: that you acknowledge/grieve your losses. To the extent that you are in denial, you block integration and feed turbulence. To the extent you acknowledge, you stop reacting, orient, and turbulence subsides. John Leiby (Acknowledgment) said:

> *Everything in life, including emotion, carries the inertia of its own momentum: Consider how an airplane glides along its trajectory for a time, even after the pilot has initiated a change in course. Similarly, as you course-correct in your own life, you might reasonably feel, for a time, that you are moving in the wrong emotional direction.*[91]

Allowing one millisecond more pain puts you in control of it. Conversely, avoiding one millisecond of pain puts it in control of you. Permitting pain supports truthfulness. Evading pain destroys integrity. You employ this principle during workouts and extreme sports, in studying for exams and competing in business, in literally every aspect of life—except when relating to your identity

---

[91] Leiby, John Samuel. *The Unpublished Lectures, 1978-1995.*

Chapter 18

Knowing That You Don't Know

As you embrace your fear, you receive reflections —awareness that is tailor-made for you and your world.

The first thought was so subtle that it went unacknowledged for hundreds of millions of years; it was in the sensations of a single cell, telling it how to maneuver and evolve. Before that, it was in the RNA that catalyzed protein,[92] but long before any of this, it was in the very nature of the universe that gave rise to life. Thought is inseparable from awareness, and awareness is inseparable from life. You may think you are the thinker of the thought, but then your thought always arises out of your relationship with what has come before.

Life emerged from the elements the moment Earth cooled from the collisions and fires of creation. As life related to the

[92] "The RNA World and the Origins of Life." *National Library of Medicine, Molecular Biology of the Cell.* 4th edition. https://www.ncbi.nlm.nih.gov/books/NBK26876/

conditions in which it found itself, it became increasingly complex. Out of complexity came the first conscious thought. It was the first "I am." Awareness becoming aware of itself.

Awareness of awareness added multi-dimensionally to consciousness. Now, thinkers could not only think of the world around them, but they could also think of themselves and the relationship of these thoughts to themselves and to other thinkers. Thoughts became increasingly important conditions in the dynamics of life. Thinkers could build thought upon thought and in so doing, effect the phenomena that gave rise to the thinker.

Thoughts changed the relationship between predator and prey and between thinkers themselves. Politics was invented, and from it, economies evolved with whole classes and subclasses of thinkers. Thinkers increasingly identified with the class and origin of their thoughts. There were good and bad thinkers, right and wrong thinkers, and right thinkers who came from the wrong places. Some thoughts could only be thought by certain thinkers. There was a lot of disagreement between the classes over this. Thinkers went to war, sacrificing their lives and the lives of their children over certain thoughts.

There were thoughts that thinkers couldn't part with because of other conflicting thoughts. Such thoughts created fears and all manner of emotional distress that required new ways of thinking to counteract. A whole new category of very esteemed thinkers arose who specialized in thinking about thinking itself. Sciences evolved and created new thoughts and new ways of relating to thoughts, and pharmaceuticals that could assuage the fears and emotions that occur when thinkers identify with the "wrong" thoughts. The very feelings from which self-awareness evolved had become the enemy of conscious thought.

Thinking that comes from thinking created a lot of confusion: Thoughts meant different things to different thinkers; some thinkers spun their thoughts in ways that deliberately confused these other thinkers. The fabric of life had become so interwoven and overladen with thought upon thought that it pretty much determined what thoughts thinkers thought about. In many ways, thinkers detached from their identities and became the thoughts themselves.

Glimpses of "I am" came and went and became increasingly painful to think about, so much so that they were avoided whenever possible. Now, thinkers were not only at war with their own thoughts and those of other thinkers but with life itself. The awesome wonder of the original awareness, the "I am" thought that gave rise to reflection and the love of understanding, became a distant and intangible memory.

Something has been lost in meaning and direction. To sort through the confusion of beliefs built around thoughts to ward off fears of past trauma, thinkers must orient around the feelings that these beliefs arose from, the fears that reinforce themselves in rituals—all the doing that is needed to avoid bad thoughts while promoting good ones. Thinkers must think "without identifying with their thoughts and without completely believing in them either." [93] They must see their

---

[93] Korzybski, A. *Science and Sanity: An Introduction to Non-Aristotelian Systems and General Semantics, Institute of General Semantics,* pp. 19, 25, 29.

thoughts arising from an evolving dynamic that they are part of. They must understand that their "thoughts never adequately describe the thing they are thinking about—that most knowing is beyond thought." [94]

Thinkers can no longer engage in thoughts that only advance their own position. They must consider life—not just their life but how their thinking fits into it all; this is because when a thought conflicts with nature, all of nature conflicts with that thought. Therefore, thinkers must become impartial. The intention must be to be true: being the truest they know to be, knowing the moment they take this position, they will discover that it is not true at all. Each time they see what is not true, they become a little less biased—more in harmony with nature.

Seeing what is not true incrementally moves you into "no thought," to being itself. But "no thought" conflicts with what life has become; truth conflicts. Not only does truth conflict, but it has also been lost. With all the manipulation, no one knows anymore what truth is. You must allow your feelings —messy as they may be— and become your own sounding board; you must discover how to *be*. The pain is in unraveling the confusion you have inherited—and unwittingly perpetuated. Life is a great paradox: part of this confusion is that you must learn lies to be true. You must learn manipulation to keep from being manipulated while not manipulating others. You must become a child in a den of wolves—starting over from scratch—questioning everything you know. You will be deceived. You will stumble.

---

[94] Ibid

As you embrace your fear, you receive reflections—awareness tailor-made for you and your world. This awareness is not contrived; it is the source of intelligence, not the product of it; it is a culmination of energy, a new creation, a phenomenon unto itself.

Awareness that creates change incorporates into every fiber of your being as you stay with what is. The attitude of "knowing that you know" reinforces conditioning and inherited perceptions; it perverts your relationship with phenomena—making the truth of it inaccessible. Questioning is the attitude of "knowing that you do not know." Knowing that you do not know incrementally moves you into relationship with the changing realities of your own involvement.

Chapter 19

Biases

Consider the possibility that you hold within yourself all of the inclinations you see in everyone around you.

Isabel was emotionally neglected as a child. Being neglected, she didn't connect well with herself and others; not connecting, others had difficulty relating to her; this "difficulty" reinforced her fear that she was "fatally flawed" in some way—so she kept her distance. [95]

Each of your beliefs and conditioned reactions takes on a life of its own, reinforcing itself and fighting for survival. The foundation is fear, and your reaction to that fear reinforces the belief that bias's perception.

Isabel's inclination to see herself as fatally flawed began long before she felt rebuffed for pestering her mother; it began with feelings she picked up as a fetus in her mother's womb, or even before—with the feelings Isabel's mother picked up as a fetus in Isabel's grandmother's womb. It is even more

---

[95] Webb, Ph.D., Jonice (2022). "Why Emotional Neglect Leaves People Feeling Flawed," *Psychology Today*. May 24. Why Emotional Neglect Leaves People Feeling Flawed | Psychology Today South Africa

convoluted: every attitude in the social structure is in Isabel and in everyone else as well.

Consider the possibility that you hold within yourself all of the inclinations you see in everyone around you. You have your ancestors, your parents, your siblings, as well as your community—all operating within you. All the extraneous agendas of the world are within you, conflicting with you and each other, pulling and pushing for support. You have become trapped in this image that all these factors have created within you. To compound your struggle, you have become complicit in presenting this image to the outside world as your true self, even as you react against its constraints upon you.

It helps to objectify the dynamic you are caught in to understand how convoluted your involvement has become. Seeing how enmeshed she was helped Isabel separate from her conditioning, allowing her to relate to the world as an autonomous person rather than as an image she held of herself that was created by others.

Awareness coming from impartial observation will work to dissolve your bias. For example, just remaining curious about the fact that you are reproaching yourself for doing something self-defeating —without reacting by adding reproach to reproach— you will notice this terrible dynamic dissipate. You may well find no fear or belief associated with the phenomenon of self-punishment, only your own self-loathing. Become curious and stay with this phenomenon, thinking, "Isn't it interesting that I am beating myself up for a decision I had no way of knowing would be an error beforehand?" or "Isn't it interesting that I hate myself?"

Identifying the phenomenon instead of being caught up in reaction allows you to observe the spectacle without adding fuel to the fire. Watch as you beat yourself up, but remain objectively curious. Noticing adds awareness and returns you to the observer self. After a time, often as little as six weeks of allowing your self-flagellation without reacting, you will notice that you are making mistakes and merely learning from them. You will have to remind yourself of how you used to beat yourself up over blunders, trivial or not.

If you can tie the development of a self-defeating belief to early relationships, that's great; biases can resolve in minutes in this way (Chapter 26, "The Three-Legged-Stool"). However, the triggers supporting self-hatred are so enmeshed in the social structure that they may not arise from a belief or condition you can easily point to, which is why staying with the feeling is so important. Stop reinforcing self-defeating dynamics by reacting against them, and they will stop triggering you.

Chapter 20

Consciousness

What you observe changes you
as it changes what you observe.

Four billion years ago, RNA catalyzed protein,[96] protein became a single cell that branched into plants and amoeba. Amoeba evolved into fish, which branched into amphibians and on to reptiles, from which mammals evolved.[97] "Fifty thousand years ago, homo sapiens found huddled in caves, making fire, and roasting meat, possessed essentially the same brain that would one day build spacecraft and land on the moon."[98]

Darwin's theory of natural selection eloquently describes how species evolved in response to the driving forces around them. His theory does not explain the experience of *being* or

---

[96] The RNA World and the Origins of Life, *National Library of Medicine, Molecular Biology of the Cell.* 4th edition: https://www.ncbi.nlm.nih.gov/books/NBK26876/

[97] Marshall, M. "Timeline: The Evolution of Life." Timeline of the evolution of life on Earth | New Scientist

[98] Ornstein, R. *The Evolution of Consciousness: Of Darwin, Freud, Cranial Fire—The Origins of the Way We Think,* p. 8, 39.

the elephant in the room: life itself. Why *life*? Why not just another chemical compound? What was it that organized elements of earth into *life*?

What we have become is too exquisite for words. How everything interrelates, builds upon, and supports everything else is beyond comprehension. You can rationalize it. You can say we are the product of a series of evolutionary accidents. You can see consciousness as a mechanical function of the brain. You can even say it is a creation of God. But whatever construction you use to explain consciousness only interferes with the sheer wonder of it. In The Genie in Your Genes, Church states:

> *We now realize that consciousness underlies and organizes matter, and not the other way around. We have discovered that changes in consciousness precipitate changes in matter. We have realized that it is consciousness that is primary and matter secondary. Consciousness is epigenetic, triggering biological expression.*[99]

Does consciousness disappear when you go to sleep, or is it everywhere and in everything? Is it a mechanical function of the brain, or does the brain merely tune into it? Is it the source of everything that is, or does everything that is create the phenomenon that we refer to as consciousness? There is much disagreement about what consciousness is or even where it is. The argument goes on with little evidence that

---

[99] Church, D. *The Genie in Your Genes, Epigenetic Medicine and the New Biology of Intention*, p. 357.

would sway one perspective to the other. Perhaps this is so because consciousness is like "the eye" in the Buddhist poem "that sees but cannot see itself."[100]

This work does not argue the theories of consciousness. It is more concerned with what consciousness does and how to place yourself in accord with it: Allowing what is to be as it is—attending to the reflections and awareness that arise from your observations. Doing so while remaining *impartial* is what consciousness requires to orient you to your *self* and your dynamic: As you observe how you are broken, you begin to mend. As you see how you are weak, you become strong. As you notice how you were foolish, you become wise. As you allow your feelings and awareness of the lack thereof—the memories, the pain, the loss, and the perceptions—you become something other. That other is always more connected, inclusive, stable, mature, and expansive.

---

[100] Author unknown

Seven Principles Of Change:

I: **Nothing is personal:** *Your experience is subject to the same laws of physics that cause clouds to appear in a clear blue sky.*

II: **Consciousness creates your experience, awareness changes consciousness:** *Whatever awareness you allow reshapes you.*

III: **Whatever you do to change reinforces the belief that is causing distress:** *Doing is the trap that drives dysfunction.*

IV: **Truth is the foundation of being:** *As you notice how you are not true, you become incrementally defined.*

V: **Meaning arises out of the relationship between form and emptiness:** *Shielding yourself from feelings closes the space through which the subtleties of life arise.*

VI**: Change is organic, unconscious, and the product of minute energy vibrations:** *In the moment you spend with what is, you are fed trillions of units of information.*

VII: **You must become the impartial observer of yourself:** *Whatever awareness you avoid works against you.*[101]

What you observe changes you
as it changes what you observe.

Change on the personal level occurs in an organic, unconscious, and, to a large extent, mechanical way. It is like a chemical reaction: when you add this to that, you get something new. You may sense the direction the reaction might take, but the product must follow the laws of physics. You can observe cause and effect, how attitudes shape your involvement, and how awareness shapes your attitudes. Change, though, occurs independently of you. It happens in the background and affects everything that is.

Consistent truthfulness about who and what you are, being present in your predicament, and the integrity to stay constructive will make you well. But how you evolve, what you become, and how what you are affects everything that is—this is of a quality unrelated to logic, words, or mind.

Awareness arises as you acknowledge your resistance and fear. Acknowledging your resistance (internal conflict) is the result of this source, working its way into alignment with what is. It is energy working against energy—a greater calm diffusing a storm. Your conflict with what is, wears you down. You resist at your peril—there is no end to the damage that can come of it.

---

[101] *The Gospel of Thomas,* The Storytellers, https://www.pbs.org/wgbh/pages/frontline/shows/religion/story/thomas.html "If you bring forth what is within you, what you bring forth will save you. If you do not bring forth what is within you, what you do not bring forth will destroy you."

When you acknowledge your resistance, the awareness that arises is not yours either—no more than seeing a sunrise makes it your sunrise. It is merely wisdom (truth) to which you now concede. So, there is nothing you can do with this new awareness. You do not even add it to memory. Consciousness adds to itself.

It is a matter of noticing as you come in and out of accord; this is the value of becoming the impartial observer of yourself—of knowing that you do not know—allowing neutrality to evolve in you; this is the value of active non-doing—allowing space for meaning to arise—the truth of things to reveal themselves; this is how you experience the unknowable sensations at the fringes of awareness and open yourself to minute increments of change.

This awareness that creates change is rarely the awareness that you are looking for. You look for light. Awareness is often of darkness—how you have misaligned around "I'm unlovable," how you manipulate to have relationships, how you lie to have a life. It all comes back upon you and adds to the storm. This awareness that creates change says, "If I give you this vision of yourself from this perspective, at this moment, and with this intensity, can you see your belief and how it sabotages your involvement? Can you see your belief as a separate element and reflect upon how you became identified with it? Can you see how your identity changes with awareness—that it has nothing to do with who you are?"

Awareness embraces the despised and lonely parts that you have spent a lifetime evading, the identity that has sabotaged you at every turn. It nurtures the unwanted inner child and shows you why you were abandoned. Grieving the why of it incorporates the esteem you were deprived of—you become less inclined to abandon others or yourself.

The question was never what you do with awareness but how it changes you. Relating differently creates different effects in life. These effects are the byproduct of consciousness building upon itself. You remember how you once were and why you were as you were, but you cannot be that person anymore.

Chapter 21

The Inner Space Traveler

There is direction, but it is the direction that comes from allowing what is to shape and orient you.

You travel inner space alone; it is the immense world within that few venture into or even acknowledge. Close your eyes and be with the vastness of it. The very worlds that exist in the cosmos exist within you. It may appear to be nothing at all, but it is where you connect with yourself. It is where all the confusion of your being oriented and coalesces. It is the space needed for who you are to arise and be identified. It encompasses all your fears and defenses and beyond these—boundless potential.

The wonderful thing about inner space is that it relates to every aspect of life. Just being with what is and staying reflective brings information from what seems to be every part of the universe. Alan Watts spoke of this phenomenon when he said: *My mind is no longer in my head; my head is in my mind.*[102]

Looking is embracing the shadow parts of yourself. In the shadows, everything you have relied upon loses validity: footprints fade, handholds lose their anchor. Venturing into your shadow self may feel like stepping off the edge of the world.

[102] Watts, A., *What is Zen,* p. 110.

However, as you visit these fearful places and see how they came into being, you begin to appreciate the wisdom of this process that gives rise to you. You let go—mind no longer spinning, unknowing of any answer or direction—open to the influences shaping you and the awareness that arises as you reflect upon these influences.

Letting go of control is the requirement of understanding. It feels misdirected at first—a loss of traction, yet letting go is aligning with the source of all creation. It helps to know that shadows are an aspect of who you are, as is this emptiness through which you feel you are falling. It is frightening to observe the immensity of your nature, frightening to let go of your belief that it is you shaping your world, and frightening to allow the experience of what you have always been doing: floating like a cottonwood seed in currents of the wind.

What you once thought was a way of progressing becomes increasingly illusory. There are no paddles to pull on, nothing to push off from. There is direction, but it is the direction that comes from allowing *what is* to shape and orient you. This new shape floats in mainstreams of increasing possibilities as awareness feeds consciousness, and consciousness feeds back upon awareness.

The leaf floating downstream no longer says, "But I wanted to land on solid ground." It is too full of wisdom learned from the stream. What tosses it to and fro? From where does turbulence come—the currents and eddies? How do the cycles repeat themselves? Nothing changes until you learn these things.

In the sparrow's first leap, the force of her own descent throws the very air against her wings that tells her who she is and how she can be.

Chapter 22

Life as The Great Teacher

As you grieve what you are not, consciousness orients around your deficiency and incrementally gives you everything you see that you are lacking.

By now, you may have a sense of how actively involved you must be—aware, mindful, and truthful—to observe without reacting. Change by not reacting is effortless—it is automatic. Your bias is starved out of existence as it is no longer being reinforced.

If you are biased, though, you can't just decide not to react. The very function of a bias is that you do react. Reacting keeps you from feeling your fear—the source of your bias. All your defenses work to keep you from experiencing this fear. Having avoided the fear, you remain unconscious of it. Your reaction keeps you from feeling the stigma of your "I'm not good enough" bias. Your reaction and the effects of your reaction are also a window to your bias and its overriding fear.

Allowing awareness is allowing your reaction to be as it is. Remain curious about your reaction—even allow yourself to react while observing your reaction. What is in you that is driving it? Do not apologize; let your change be the apology. Let the social dissonance, even the loss of friendship resulting from your reaction, motivate you to get relative to the source of it. Stop throwing yourself under the bus. Be with what you are. Find ways to exaggerate your bias rather than mitigate it. Let life teach!

Notice how shame is triggered—and guilt, how you apologize for your reaction to get over your shame and are then forgiven. Your own manipulation sabotages awareness: You promise never to react again to a fear your reaction helped you to forget.

Can you see the discipline, impartiality—and maturity required? If you choose this path, you must cultivate an appreciation of these traits. Each time you notice how you lack maturity, you incrementally gain it.

Again, none of this is anything that you can do. It is a matter of allowing awareness to grow, mindfully noticing what you do and do not do, what you are and what you are not—and why. Do not write it down. Life will remind you time and again, in the real-time moment of each situation.

Change does not come from what you remember or force yourself to do. It does not come from affirmation, visualization, journaling, analyzing, belief, or spiritual practice. Instead, change comes from grieving every nuance of what you allow yourself to see that you are not—without taking any of it personally. As you grieve what you are not, consciousness orients around your deficiency and incrementally gives you everything you see that you are lacking—you become it.

Affirmations, beliefs, and journaling are just your sneaky ways of avoiding the pain of being with what is, and with who and what you are now. You are the tablet life is writing upon. Being with what is, you begin to orient—you begin to change. As you begin to change, what you just believed, what you just affirmed, what you just wrote down is no longer relevant. This is the real-time incorporation of information that I'm talking about; the writing of it keeps you stuck.

Chapter 23

Subjective Reality

Whatever you do reinforces whatever you do.

The social structure says you can choose any way of *being* that you like. So, you choose happy, but choosing "happy" is not what happiness is, at least until you choose it. Because the moment you choose happiness, "choosing happy" becomes your reality, as opposed to the experience of a well-tended child who is naturally vibrant and affectionate.

It's confusing because whatever you do reinforces whatever you do and shapes your reality. When you choose happy, you reinforce all of your inherited assumptions and beliefs about what happy is; this gives a sense of direction—even a change in mood. However, the well-tended child is the product of an organic phenomenon rather than an arbitrary choice. He or she experiences enthusiasm and delight without any of the beliefs associated with your concept of "happy."

Your orientation to the world began in your mother's womb as chemical reactions to her stresses and joys. As stated (Chapter 10, "Your Intangible Self"), genes are activated or silenced by feelings and sensations experienced by the individual. It is entirely impersonal. The evolving configuration, you, is precisely orchestrated for survival in the world you are about to enter. The world you are about to enter is full of trauma, but it is also about life, and life works to orient you to optimum benefit through the *impartial* experience of this very trauma.

That is, as you impartially experience the feeling/attitude that motivated your "happy" choice, the underlying beliefs and social conditioning associated with your perception begin to dissolve; you enter an undefined space, which is aliveness itself; this is what you bypass when you "choose" happy.

Everyone evolves a slightly different perception and so reacts differently, with slightly different ways of coping with the stress and fear of inherited trauma. Our way of coping becomes a conditioned reaction that, over time, eliminates awareness of our inherited trauma.

As a result, we become very protective of our coping strategy—we even identify with it. We take criticism of how we cope quite personally; it is a visceral reaction—as much of an evolution as our hand or foot. Our visceral reaction shows us that the inherited trauma/identity/fear is still operating within us. However, we have learned so many ways of defending against it that, to our conscious mind, fear does not, for the most part, exist. So, even though we do not feel the stress of our fear, we remain quite stressed by all the coping that is required to avoid awareness of it. Your condition, your perception, and your reality is reinforced by everything you do to avoid awareness of it; this is how the unconscious coping that began in our mothers' womb evolves into a life of stuck-ness.

It does not matter if your way of coping appears very similar to your partner's way of coping. Everyone's way of coping, it seems, is a source of estrangement from everyone else. This is because coping evades whatever issue is involved. You can appreciate how "getting busy," for example, helps me get past my depression, but "busy" also gets me past personal issues and, as a result, connection with myself and you.

Each of us enters this world in a unique cocoon of self-reinforcing reality;[103] [104] this reality evolves to mitigate our stressors and fears. When what we do to alleviate our fear seems to alleviate our fear, our perceived reality is reinforced, even when what we do has no tangible relationship to our fear. I refer back to the example of the rituals and beliefs of the 1950s headhunting Asmat tribes of New Guinea to ward off sickness and death (Chapter 3, "Nothing Is Personal"). It's the distraction our doing creates, or the intention itself (what we believe our doing does), that gets reinforced. Also, the context of our doing reinforces what we do: Smoking while driving, for example, conditions the need for a cigarette every time you get behind the wheel.

---

[103] Why We Think Perception Is Reality – Perception is a Reflection of You, Seeker Project 4 Spiritual Exploration (SP4SE), *Techniques For Exploring Consciousness*: https://seekerproject4se.org/2023/08/16/why-we-think-perception-is-reality-perception-is-a-reflection-of-you-an-individually-crafted-fiction/#:~:text=What%20we%20perceive%20is%20subject%20to%20various%20cognitive,is%20reality%2C%20and%20their%20reality%20cannot%20be%20questioned

[104] Hoffman, Donald. "Do we see reality as it is?" https://www.youtube.com/watch?v=oYp5XuGYqqY

Everything you arise out of, everything you do in response, the why, how, where, when, what, and with whom of it, reinforces everything about you: your identity, how you relate, your perception—your reality. Each action tied to some perceived benefit becomes a consciousness all its own—looking for ways to reinforce its existence—even when its survival is counter to your own.[105]

There is an alternative: Take the position of not knowing what happiness is, or even how to achieve it—of allowing the impartial experiencing of your fears and reactions to dissolve their underlying beliefs and conditioning. This practice orients you more precisely around life's vicissitudes than you could ever surmise. It takes courage that you may not yet have to step out of inherited perceptions and into an evolving reality. It may take hand-holding and the wisdom and encouragement of those who have gone before; this is the intention for the following chapter, "Maturity."

---

[105] Schwartz Ph.D., Richard C. (2018). *Greater Than The Sum Of Our Parts. Discovering Your True Self Through Internal Family Systems Therapy*. Sounds True.

Chapter 24

Maturity

You never know when and under what circumstances your inner five-year-old will jump out. [106]

Many years ago, I participated in group therapy. The therapist interacted with us by asking each individual, in turn, "How did your week go?" Unfortunately, this approach was not conducive to meaningful dialogue, because it didn't allow participants to respond to any particular individual's statement. However, as is often the case, human nature overcame the obstacle and forced the dialogue that needed to occur.

Unstructured sharing supports personal growth in a very dynamic way. Jackie may say something that has meaning to Jose across the room. Jose's observation touches Blake, and Blake's reflection prompts an awareness in Chris of conditioning she had been reacting to unconsciously. Her response might interpose something poignant that moves the conversation in a new and surprisingly meaningful direction.

This is what happened with this group. While all this interplay between individual participants was going on, the

[106] Leiby, John Samuel, *The Unpublished Lectures,* 1978-1995

silent group members listened to what was being shared, made connections to their lives, and considered what they might contribute. Awareness develops, and consciousness builds in real-time. In group dynamics such as this, everyone evolves, whether they speak or not.

In this session, the totality of what these individuals shared in their protected vulnerability exposed a microcosm of all human interactions. The members of the group immediately sensed their interrelatedness. Interjections were offered spontaneously from different sides of the room—each sharing built upon another's perception. When such breakthroughs occur, the savvy group leader surrenders control and allows the exchange to continue organically; this is what the therapist leading this group chose to do, and it served the group members very successfully.

The following week, Daren shared, "When I attend groups like this, I often get a small sense of myself and lose it the moment I leave the room. But last week, I got a really strong sense of myself; I've held on to it all week, and I'd like to build upon what we did." Several others nodded in agreement, and the room filled with anticipation. Unstructured groups of individuals openly sharing their lives, awareness, and feelings with the intention of self-discovery can profoundly support personal growth.

Specifically, this woman's leap in identity arose from relating truthfully to an indirect question. Cayman had said, "I think Daren is avoiding me." I asked, "Daren, are you avoiding Cayman?" As she scooted to the edge of her seat, Daren took a moment and said, "Well, yes, I am. Our eyes met as Cayman came up the stairs, and I smiled. I was glad to see

Cayman, but I think he's been trying to get me to smile at him again ever since, and I feel like I give myself away when I do that."

I asked Cayman. "Are you trying to get Daren to smile at you?" Cayman flushed sheepishly and said, "Yes, I guess I am." Daren's reality was confirmed, and we all saw our unspoken influence on each other. Her exceptional growth occurred with a few moments of identification instead of numerous, perhaps, years of therapy sessions.

Unstructured groups support connection, intimacy, and identity; with such dynamics, growth, and maturity are "a given." Truthfulness supports the intensity of what is shared. Intensity helps incorporate what is seen; when someone shares intimately, all members feel valued. The dynamics of unstructured sharing groups support meaningful change; all we need to do is pay attention.

Such groups ideally begin with a bit of ritual: a candle in the center of the room, a chime to invoke focus, and a moment of stillness. They then proceed with a discussion that arises organically from the participants' reflections. These may include statements regarding awareness of a dynamic in their lives, confusion, conflicts, feelings, or perceptions occurring at the moment; this supports a theme that is always relevant and flows naturally into expressions of curiosity and discovery. No one knows if or when they may speak, so everyone relates to what is being shared.

Once the sharing begins, the leadership is in the hands of the group. Whoever volunteers to start the group is responsible for ending it at an agreed-upon time, usually with the last call for a summation by participants. An hour and a half to two hours is required to develop and expand upon a subject with eight to twelve people. Groups of more than sixteen can repel rather than attract participants and should, therefore, consider splitting into two groups. Encouraging members to take turns leading the group promotes ownership; it also develops leadership skills, which are helpful for such eventualities as when groups get too large and need to split into smaller ones.

Themes offered to "get the group talking" only sidetrack meaningful sharing, spinning the discussion toward the topical, intellectual, and issues of opinion. A great deal of inertia is generated, which is difficult to overcome when an arbitrary question such as "Tell us what you are grateful for?" is imposed. Such suggestions result in everyone focusing on what they will say when it is their turn to speak—instead of the thoughtful relating that occurs in an evolving conversation.

Everything we do reinforces everything we do: Arbitrary themes offered to "get the group talking" create the need for arbitrary themes to "get the group talking." However, encouraging participants to take responsibility for observing themselves throughout the week for subjects to bring forward supports presence and relevant sharing. The social structure is constantly orchestrating our thoughts. The practice of awareness requires subjects that arise from within.

The relevance of a given subject is more important than the subject itself. The effect is multi-dimensional: when you relate to "what is," anger —and many other problems—dissipates. Change occurs when relevant information is incorporated in real-time—whether or not you are aware of this phenomenon. Nevertheless, the more present you are, the more profound the transformation. By their nature, sharing groups support the mindfulness that relevant information arises from and the presence that incorporates awareness.

Every group member needs to commit to allowing relevant subjects to evolve. The commitment must be to sit silently throughout the session, if necessary, rather than going topical or to subjects of opinion. Topical subjects are popular because they bypass the vulnerability of self-discovery. Silence permits subjects to percolate. There are many forces at work in any group; meaningful subjects require time for individuals to formulate and position themselves around.

Each participant must learn to act as a sounding board. If the subject draws you in, it is relevant; if attendees have to work to keep it going, it is not. It is self-defeating to add energy to an irrelevant subject by talking. Let it die, or identify it as a subject that does not resonate with you; this adds relevance to the group dynamic and allows it to move more meaningfully. Do you see the definition that must evolve in you to identify a subject that does not resonate? Unstructured sharing is a way of maturing dynamically in real-time.

If this concept interests you, the afterword of this book invites you to join a **FREE** virtual sharing or perhaps a brick-and-mortar group sponsored by someone, maybe you, in your area.

Inevitably, there are situations in life where you are caught off guard—overwhelmed by figures in authority positions who question and harangue you in ways that make you feel small.

Notice and be with your reaction—whatever the anger or argument. The dynamics entrapping you are not unlike those you experienced as a child; the same relative power is being exerted over you.

Staying with your immaturity in these situations gives you the dignity to be more with yourself—not only the next time you experience the feeling of being overpowered but in everything you are and do from now on.

You never know when and under what circumstances your inner five-year-old will jump out.[107] When you shift responsibility and make excuses, that immature part of you will jump out even more. That is how life/consciousness works: The phenomena creating your immature response will continue to develop within and around you until you identify and relate to it.

Maturity does not come from wealth or position. It does not come from taking on responsibility (e.g., marriage, children). It does not come from "fake it till you make it." Maturity comes from incrementally allowing into awareness all the ways that you are not mature. You find it in your fears, your inhibitions, your defeating self-image, your defensiveness, shame, and the need to be right. You find it in your interpersonal conflicts, emotional disturbance, feelings of futility, co-dependence, and depression. The wounded and discarded consciousness remains, waiting to be accepted—to be seen and understood, the same consideration you have wanted others to give you.[108]

---

[107] Leiby, John Samuel, *The Unpublished Lectures,* 1978-1995

[108] "Internal Family Systems Therapy," Editors, *Psychology Today*, 05/20/22: https://www.psychologytoday.com/us/therapy-types/internal-family-systems-therapy,

Chapter 25

Conscious Evolution

What you allow fills you in;
what you withhold hollows you out.

Your body is made of calcium, potassium, carbon, and water, but you are none of these. You have thoughts and awareness, but you are not those either. The essence that is you is intangible and always changing, so it cannot be defined. You have logic, but this ability evolved organically and unconsciously, and most of what you are is not logical. Logic builds cars, bridges, and airplanes—but it does not build you. Your identity and sense of self developed unwittingly from genetics and early relationships. Your evolution from the elements is of an intelligence beyond the mind. Mind did not create this intelligence; intelligence created this mind. You are a product of one consciousness relating to another, each incrementally building upon the other in real-time.

You are fundamentally a sensing creature. You learned to define feelings with words; now you use words to distract you from your feelings. Everything you think, do, and believe reinforces itself and sends you down a random path. This path is fantasy; it has nothing to do with what is—nothing to do with being. When you try to figure it out, logic diverts you even further; it wears you down and creates your worst fears.

Logic places you in a virtual world. You play on the field of "unlovable." You counter unlovable with "I am too lovable," or "God made me. Therefore, I'm lovable!" You are so obsessed with counteracting your stigma that you trade one belief for another without ever questioning the validity of either.

"Desire obscures anxiety and reinforces controls. Controls build upon controls until you are stifled and shut down." [109] You become overwhelmed with remembering what to do when, instead of being the person who spontaneously aligns with what is—the person who gladly incorporates deficiencies, immaturities, and mistakes into their arising self. It is in knowing that you do not know that you experience presence. The gift is in seeing what you are not, and permitting life to teach you.

Trying to be how you think you "should" be, punishes you; it is your mind arguing with itself, reinforcing fragmentation—further incorporating the qualities you dislike. Your maturity is trapped at the age you were when you began repressing your feelings. Now, you are an adult triggered and wounded by every slight —real and imagined—everything sticks to you. Your ego is a ball of defense reactions and power plays. You fill your loneliness with wants, ambitions, and endless doing.

You believe you are insufficient, but this is because you are afraid to allow what you are not to teach you. You are

---

[109] Watts, A. *The Way of Zen*, p. 136-138.

afraid because you take what you have become personally, and you take what you have become personally, because you are afraid. You are bound by the thoughts you use to control your feelings.

You unconsciously became what you are as an organic response to everything that is. While you were avoiding this, you were becoming that. It was not your fault: your empty parts are the reflection of adolescent fears. Your fears are the identity you fight against, but neither this identity nor the vision you hold for yourself has anything to do with who you are.

You undo the damage by reversing how it occurred: by incrementally opening yourself to the feelings that overwhelmed you in infancy. If you wish to mend the broken pieces, you must align with what is. The teaching, the discipline, the practice—all of this is in the "being with." When you grieve what is, consciousness incrementally learns how to fill in the empty spaces and build in you what has so long been missing.

Building upon what is missing is complex. It requires patience, maturity, and wisdom. Constructive change requires incorporating what you are not. If this were not the case, you would not need the change. You become increasingly constructive as you impartially observe how and why you injure yourself: Noticing how you choose the path of least resistance and how you are identified with negativity, while not taking any of it personally, will build in you the wisdom needed to learn from the discomfort of your predicament.

The social structure feeds off of devastation and actively promotes it, so do not be disheartened when change seems slow. In such a world, a quarter inch of integration is a mega-achievement, but each change builds exponentially upon the last, organically affecting every part of you. In the moment you spend with what is, you are fed trillions of units of information. Looking back, you will be amazed by the profundity of your transformation and the short time in which it occurred. Lifetime biases can vaporize in a single moment of introspection.

Fear is the field you play upon, but as you allow your fear, the perimeter walls that have defined your world dissolve, and you expand exponentially— "unlovable" becomes irrelevant. You begin letting go of the mind. Understanding comes not by "thinking" but by "being with," by allowing energy to orient and coalesce. Whatever awareness you allow reshapes you—no thought required. What you allow fills you in; what you withhold hollows you out. As you change, those around you change, they have to because you are integral to all that is. You are aligned with the intelligence from which everything evolved—beyond the mind.

Chapter 26

The Three-Legged-Stool

Allowing awareness changes your dynamic —you find yourself in a new paradigm with a new you.

Several years ago, I met the woman of my dreams. We went to lunch with friends, and I sat across from her. She learned that I had been a contractor and asked if I would come to her home and give her some input on a project. It was a fantastic opportunity to get acquainted. All I had to do was reach into my pocket and hand her my card, but I feared I would disintegrate right in front of her if I did that. "She does not know that I'm not a substantial person," kept running through my mind. I felt such conflict and dread that I got up and walked out on her without a word. I sat in my vehicle, overwhelmed with confusion, thinking, "What's WRONG with me?" I had vague recollections of this phenomenon occurring throughout my life, which I had compulsively ignored, but I couldn't let this one go. I stayed with it for weeks while walking in my neighborhood, particularly at night.

I concluded that I had to know the truth of my belief that I was defective. I was sure I was defective because, throughout my life, everything I reached for disintegrated just before I touched it. When a teacher asked, "Who has the answer?" and I raised my hand, the answer vanished the moment she called my name. It was an incredibly frightening and shameful aspect of myself to explore, and so I had avoided this belief my entire life.

One night, when I couldn't sleep, I imagined asserting myself—reaching for something with my right hand and saying, "I want this." As I reached, something else—my left hand rose and took my assertion apart. This dynamic surprised me because it seemed mechanical and without any intention or expectation that I could find coming from me—yet it was coming entirely from me.

I tried the exercise again with the same result. What was this thing that took my assertion apart? I stayed open. I suspected it was my conditioning—but how and from where? The moment I allowed the question, my reflection took me back forty years, living as a young adult with my father. I repeatedly stood up to my father in those days to gain his acceptance. However, I found myself helpless in these encounters. He had a way of deriding me with just one look, a tactic he had used from my earliest memory. It only took a second, and I disintegrated.

Each time this occurred, I would be overwhelmed with the knowledge that it would take at least six weeks for me to pull myself together again, at which point we would repeat this cycle. Back then, I thought my perseverance would eventually make me strong enough to withstand my father's scorn, and force him to relate to me person to person. But this maneuver only served to re-injure me and so this scenario continued until I left home.

I retraced my steps:

As I began my assertion, I felt a tinge of apprehension.

"What is this apprehension?" I wondered.

"Well, I fear I will disintegrate if I assert myself."

"Is there any other fear?" I asked the universe.

"Yes," came the answer, "I will see that I am defective."

As my imaginary right hand reached as high as it could, a conditioned hand rose from my left side and dissolved my assertion. I thought this dynamic was curious. What if my disappointments throughout life resulted from my fear and its conditioned reaction? What if my reaction to my fear reinforced my belief/identity and my identity—mirrored back by myself and those around me—reinforced my fear?

Maybe I'm not defective after all, I thought. I repeated this exercise, beginning with my apprehension at asserting myself.

"Is there a fear?"

"Yes," came the answer, "that I'll disintegrate if I assert myself."

"Is there a reaction?"

"Yes, it is my apprehension about asserting myself."

"Is there a belief?"

"Yes, that I am defective."

"Is there a conditioned response?"

"Yes, it's dissolving my assertion as I assert it."

As I came around to the big, "I'm defective" belief, belief in my defectiveness vaporized. It just dissolved—blew up right in front of me, and I immediately gained what felt like 25% more mental capacity.

This surprised me. I asserted myself again, thinking, "I want this!"—but felt no apprehension. As I reached for my imaginary desire, nothing arose to take my assertion apart. I followed my assertion around and found no belief in my defectiveness.

Could I remember my belief? Yes.

Could I identify with it? No!

In three and a half minutes of looking, a very crippling, lifelong dynamic became irrelevant. Since that night, I have had no trouble asserting myself.

Figure 2: *The Cycle of Impartial Self-Observation: as you impartially observe your fear, belief, and conditioned reaction—how each reinforces the other—your dynamic becomes increasingly constructive.*

Notice that I didn't do anything to change. I simply observed David to see what David does. I observed the dynamic that David was caught in. I stayed reflective and considered, "What contributes to David being as he is?" I allowed my fear without reacting. I couldn't do anything to interfere with how my experiment unfolded because if I did, I knew I would only bypass awareness and reinforce my fear; I would never know the truth of it. I simply allowed awareness to enter my fear-filled and shame-based dynamic. Consciousness changed.

The stool's three legs, referred to in this chapter's title, relate to your fear, belief, and conditioned reaction. The seat of the stool is a dynamic like that of "Family," from which these three legs evolved and received credibility. Identifying any of these three legs while staying with that identification —allowing it to be as it is without reacting— adds awareness while removing your participation.

Removing your participation undermines the dynamic that gives rise to the leg, like belief in a self-defeating identity, such as in my "I'm defective" example. If you stay with your fear without reacting, it becomes less intimidating. If you identify a self-defeating belief without reacting, it stops being reinforced, gradually loses credibility, and fades into irrelevance. If you identify your conditioning without reacting, the seat of the stool receives less and less support as you increasingly understand how you participate in your dilemma.

As you *impartially* relate to any of the three legs, your relationship to the dynamic begins to change. For example, you find yourself needing less approval. This happens as the belief leg — "I'm not good enough" — begins to dissolve. Since a three-legged stool cannot stand on two legs, your dynamic must change. When your self-defeating belief fades, your fear fades, and with it, your conditioning fades. In whatever order you relate to it, a given dynamic cannot function as it has without all its parts. Allowing awareness changes the components of your dynamic, and you find yourself in a new paradigm with a new you.

The Three-Legged-Stool

***Figure 3** The Concept of the Three-Legged Stool: as you relate to any one of the three legs of the stool without reacting, your self-defeating dynamic collapses.*

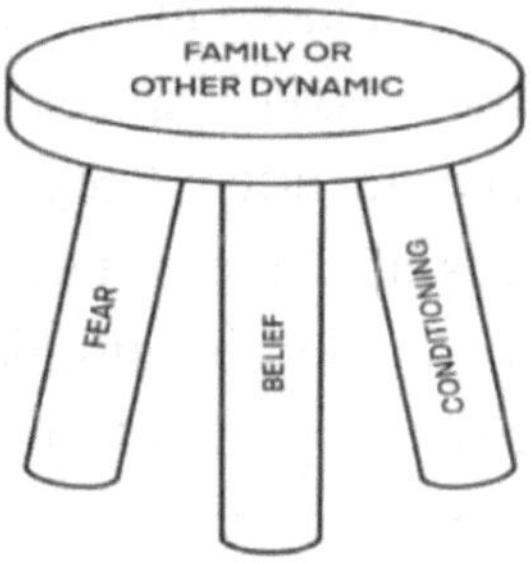

I have used the three-legged stool concept to relate to numerous beliefs, fears, and conditioned reactions with the same result. The dilemma troubling me, whether it is a fear, belief, my conditioning, or the dynamic out of which these arose, cannot sustain itself without my reaction to it.

If you identify a fear, belief, and conditioned reaction and observe how each reinforces the other, as in my "I'm defective" example, you can get relative to your biased perception much quicker. Noticing how this dynamic evolved early on and observing yourself in its context also helps separate you from your conditioning.

Trapped in my belief, I had no way of knowing if I was defective or not. Throughout my life, mistakes reinforced my identity, and my reactions reinforced my belief/fear. I was 99% sure that I truly was defective. All I could do was observe myself without contaminating my observation with a reaction, without doing or thinking anything that would support or counteract my belief. I could only achieve neutrality by consistently noticing when and how I was not neutral—when I did react.

Do you see how adding aspects of relativity —seeing how one thing relates to and is dependent upon another for its reality— undermined the belief in my defectiveness? Do you see the myriad attributes simultaneously incorporated — courage, identity, integrity— as I allowed and observed my feelings of defectiveness? I must embody my father's scorn: the shame and humiliation of it—welcoming my triggers as sources of good information, as opposed to shutting them down with a reaction. Do you see the myriad points of relativity that were added to consciousness by experiencing and grieving the nuances of my humiliation? When I did react, I had to reflect upon what fear/belief my reaction reinforced, without doing or thinking anything that would support or counteract my belief, my reaction to it, or the conditions from which these arose. Do you see how not doing anything to prove or disprove my fear allowed it to dissipate? When I saw that I reacted, I merely gave this awareness to consciousness; there was more work for it to do. Do you see the change that occurred when I noticed that I reacted? I was incrementally moving from unconscious to conscious.

Chapter 27

Don't Read This Book

You are the book you must read.

David Hawkins in his book, *Letting Go,* presents a litany of methodologies designed to "help" you. He suggests, among a great many other things, that:

> *When upset, you go to a doctor or psychiatrist, an analyst, a social worker, or an astrologer. You take up religion, get philosophy, take the Erhard Seminar Training (est), tap yourself with EFT.*[110] *You get your chakras balanced, try some reflexology, go for ear acupuncture, do iridology, get healed with lights and crystals.* [111]

Each methodology evolves from a different motive, reality, philosophy, or belief. For some, it is a distraction—the avoidance of pain. Others do not focus on their pain but rather

[110] Tap the meridians around your head, underarms, and chest, using the Emotional Freedom Technique, while reciting an affirmation.
[111] Hawkins, D. R. *Letting Go: Pathway of Surrender*, p. 2.

the source of it. Some seek psychological remedies, others philosophical ones. Some pursue healing from without; for others, it is from within. For some, the answer is in the spiritual and otherworldly—enlightenment. For most, the "solution" is an endless random quest.

I agree with Hawkins that the solution needs to be "self-evident … requiring no dependence upon dogma, belief, practice, or practitioner." Methodologies are created to solve problems—one-size-fits-all cookie cutters for dealing with this or that. But life is organic and evolutionary, not a formula or problem to be solved—it is not logical. Methodologies regiment and distract you from discovery: while practicing this, you overlook that.

You could add another hundred pages to this list of Hawkins's—things you could do to "help" yourself, and no doubt many would be helpful. However, it is important to note that as vital as foundational learning is, the attention you give to a teacher, guru, coach, therapist, motivational speaker, spiritual practice, or methodology takes attention away from you. Ultimately, you are the book you must read, the class you must take, the guru you must study under, and the subject in which you must earn a doctorate to discover the nuances of you.

Your interpersonal difficulties speak volumes about your skill and motivation to avoid yourself or, as someone once said, "to avoid the pain of your false identity." The only way to work through the nuances of you is to painstakingly observe what you do and why you do it without reinforcing your dynamic by reacting against it. You must bring to awareness all the ways you are not impartial to allow the quality of impartiality to evolve in you.

You must judge what you do with ruthless objectivity while not taking any of it personally and not sabotaging your judgment with the judgment of others. You can only do this by noticing when you do look away, when you do take things personally, and when you do judge wrongly. You must be able to observe and *impartially* criticize yourself. Because, when you see how you are wrong, you know more about how to be right. When you acknowledge that you don't understand, you begin to. Moreover, when you notice that you behaved like a five-year-old but did not excuse, shame, or blame—you mature.

Afterword

If unstructured sharing interests you, I invite you to join a **FREE** virtual sharing group at **DiscoverTheSelf.com.** There, you can contribute to a culture where self-observation, facing one's fears, and personal growth are the norm. You can also sign up for physical groups sponsored by volunteers (maybe you?) in your area.

If this book speaks to you, **PLEASE** write reviews on **Amazon,** and **Goodreads**. A statement about your honest experience will help others find this work.

Thank you for taking the time to share in these perspectives.

Bibliography

"At What Age is the Brain Fully Developed?" Mental Health Daily,2015. https://mentalhealthdaily.com/2015/02/18/at-what-age-is-the-brain-fully-developed/

Busentiz, N. "How many people died in the Inquisition?" (2015).The Cripplegate.com, February 28th. https://thecripplegate.com/how-many-people-died-in-the-inquisition/

Carpenter, Arthur (2017). "The U. S. Has Been At War 222 out of 239 Years," Hypotheses Freakonometrics, March. https://freakonometrics.hypotheses.org/50473

Chen, Yijing , Jinying, Xu, Chen, Yu, Ruggiero Francavilla (2021) Academic Editor, "Regulation of Neurotransmitters by the Gut Microbiota and Effects on Cognition in Neurological Disorders," The National Library of Medicine, Jun 19. https://pmc.ncbi.nlm.nih.gov/articles/PMC8234057/

"China shames jaywalkers through facial recognition," (2017) Phys.Org, June 20. https://phys.org/news/2017-06-china-shames-jaywalkers-facial-recognition.html

Bibliography

Choi, Boungho, Park, Soowon (2021). "Bullying Perpetration, Victimization, and Low Self-esteem: Examining Their Relationship Over Time," National Library of Medicine, Jan 11. https://pubmed.ncbi.nlm.nih.gov/33428081/

Church, D. (2009). The Genie in Your Genes, Epigenetic Medicine and the New Biology of Intention, 2nd ed. Energy Psychology Press.

"Cognitive Development in the Teen Years." Stanford Children's Health/Lucile Packard Children's Hospital. https://www.stanfordchildrens.org/en/topic/default?id=cognitive-development-in-adolescence-90-P01594

Crawford, Christina (1978). Mommy Dearest, William Morrow.

David, E. J. R. Ph.D. (2015). "Internalized Oppression: We Need to Stop Hating Ourselves." Psychology Today, September 30th. https://www.psychologytoday.com/us/blog/unseen-and-unheard/201509/internalized-oppression-we-need-stop-hating-ourselves

Dean, J. (2008). "When the Self Emerges: Is That Me in the Mirror." Psyblog, http://www.spring.org.uk/2008/05/when-self-emerges-is-that-me-in-mirror.php.

Bibliography

"Evolution of Birds." Libre Texts Biology, https://bio.libretexts.org/Bookshelves/Introductory_and_General_Biology/General_Biology_(Boundless)/29%3A_Vertebrates/29.05%3A_Birds/29.5B%3A_Evolution_of_Birds

"Evolution of Amphibians & Reptiles," The Paleozoic Era, Scared Cricket: http://www.michellecaldwell.com/linkfiles/scaredcricket/articles/other/evolution.html

"Form and Emptiness." Purified Mind. http://www.purifymind.com/FormEmp.html

Gastroenterol, Ann, Carabotti, Marilia, Scirocco, Annunziata, Maselli, Maria Antonietta, Seven, Carola (2015). "The gut-brain axis: interactions between enteric microbiota, central and enteric nervous systems," *Annals of Gastroenterology,* Apr-Jun. https://www.ncbi.nlm.nih.gov/pmc/articles/PMC4367209/

Gecas, Viktor and Seff, Monica A. (1990). "Social Class and Self-Esteem: Psychological Centrality, Compensation, and the Relative Effects of Work and Home." Social Psychology Quarterly. https://www.jstor.org/stable/2786677

Gillian, James (2003). Shame (2021). Guilt, and Violence, 70(4). The John Hopkins University Press. https://www.jstor.org/stable/40971965

Bibliography

Gunnarsson, Nina Veetnisha (2021). "The Self-perpetuatung Cycle of Shame and Self-injury," Humanity & Society. 45(3): 313.333. https://journals.sagepub.com/doi/pdf/10.1177/0160597620904475

Hanh, T. N. (2012). "The Heart Sutra: The Fullness of Emptiness." Lion's Roar, https://www.lionsroar.com/heart-sutra-fullness-emptiness/

Hawkins, D. R. (2013). Letting go: Pathway of Surrender. Hay House.

"Historical Trauma and cultural healing," University of Minnesota Extension, Reviewed, 2020. https://extension.umn.edu/trauma-and-healing/historical-trauma-and-cultural-healing

Hoefer, David L. "Conditioning." Discover the Self, 2012. https://discovertheself.com/conditioning/

Hoffman, Carl (2014). Savage Harvest: A Tale of Cannibals, Colonialism and Michael Rockefeller's Tragic Quest for Primitive Art, William Morrow. pp. 34 36.

Hoffman, Donald, "Do we see reality as it is?" https://www.youtube.com/watch?v=oYp5XuGYqqY

"How Dinosaurs Shrank and Became Birds?" Quanta Magazine, https://www.quantamagazine.org/how-birds-evolved-from-dinosaurs-20150602/

Bibliography

"How Intergenerational Trauma Impacts Families," Psych Central, Medical Review, April, 2022. https://psychcentral.com/lib/how-intergenerational-trauma-impacts-families#family-impact

Hurley, D. (2013). "Grandma's Experiences Leave a Mark on Your Genes." Discover Magazine, June. https://amackeydesign.com/trait-vs-fate-epigenetics"

"Inquisition, Editors." History.com, November, 2017. https://www.history.com/topics/religion/inquisition

"Internal Family Systems Therapy," Editors, Psychology Today, 05/20/22; https://www.psychologytoday.com/us/therapy-types/internal-family-systems-therapy

Jones, R. S. (2007). "Reversing the Irreversible," Nature 450, November 14. 357-359. https://www.nature.com/articles/450357a

Khazan, O. (2018). "Inherited Trauma Shapes Your Health." The Atlantic, October 16, 2018. https://www.theatlantic.com/health/archive/2018/10/trauma-inherited-generations/573055/

Kinross, James M, Darzi, Ara W., Nicholson, Jeremy K. (2011). "Gut microbiome-host interactions in health and disease," Genome Medicine, 04 March. https://genomemedicine.biomedcentral.com/articles/10.1186/gm228

Korzybski, A. (2010). "Science and Sanity: An Introduction to Non-Aristotelian Systems and General Semantics." Institute of General Semantics.

Kraus, Michael W. and Park, Jun W (2014). "The Undervalued self: social class and self-evaluation," Frontiers in Psychology 05 December. https://www.frontiersin.org/articles/10.3389/fpsyg.2014.01404/full

Krisch, Joshua A. (2023). "The Five Stages Of Self-Awareness Explain When Babies Recognize Themselves In The Mirror." Fatherly, July 28. The 5 Stages Of Self-Awareness Explain What Babies See In The Mirror

Lansford, Jennifer E., Miller-Johnson, Shari, Berlin, Dodge, Kenneth A, Bates and Pettit (2007). "Early Physical Abuse and Later Violent Delinquency: A Prospective Longitudinal Study," PubMed Central, Aug. https://www.ncbi.nlm.nih.gov/pmc/articles/PMC2771618/

Leiby, J. S. The Unpublished Lectures.

Lipton, B. H. (2015). The Biology of Belief: Unleashing the Power *of Consciousness, Matter & Miracles.* Hay House.

Bibliography

Lynch, Jonathan B. and Hsiao, Elaine Y. (2023). "Toward understanding links between the microbiome and neurotransmitters," *Annals of the New York Academy of Sciences,* April 5. https://nyaspubs.onlinelibrary.wiley.com/doi/10.1111/nyas.14993

Lyons, Barry, Gibson, Matthew, Dolezal, Luna (2018). "Stories of Shame," The Lancet, April 21. https://www.thelancet.com/journals/lancet/article/PIIS0140-6736%2818%2930897-3/fulltext

Magee, Dr. Mike, (2006). "The Catholic Inquisition, Methods Of Torture And Victims," Church and State, June 1. https://churchandstate.org.uk/2022/06/the-catholic-inquisition-methods-of-torture-and-victims

Marshall, M. (2009). "Timeline: The Evolution of Life." New Scientist. https://www.newscientist.com/article/dn17453-timeline-the-evolution-of-life/

"Newton's laws of motion," Webster Dictionary. https://www.merriam-webster.com/dictionary/impartially

Mitchell, Stephen, Lao Tsu, Tao Te Ching, Harper & Row, 1988. P. 11.

Nichols, Robert G and Davenport, Emily R (2020). "The relationship between the gut microbiome and host gene expression: A review," *The National Institute of Health*, Nov 22. https://pmc.ncbi.nlm.nih.gov/articles/PMC7680557/pool

Ornstein, R. (991). The Evolution of Consciousness: Of Darwin, Freud, Cranial Fire—The Origins of the Way We Think. Prentice Hall Press.

Peterson, J. (2010). The Necessity of Virtue. https://www.youtube.com/watch?v=gwUJHNPMUyU&t=

Pine, R. (Translation.). The Heart Sutra. Counterpoint, 2004.

Proal, Amy D, Lindseth, Inge A. and Marshall, Trevor G (2017). "Microbe microge and host-microbe interactions drive microbiome dysbiosis and inflammatory processes," Pub Med, Jan;23. https://pubmed.ncbi.nlm.nih.gov/28245427/

Riebeek, H. (2009). "The History of an Idea That Launched the Scientific Revolution," Planetary Motion. https://earthobservatory.nasa.gov/features/OrbitsHistory

Bibliography

Rodriguez, T. (2015). "Descendants of Holocaust Survivors Have Altered Stress Hormones." Scientific American. https://www.scientificamerican.com/article/descendants-of-holocaust-survivors-have-altered-stress-hormones/

Schwartz, Richard C. Ph.D. 2018). Greater Than The Sum Of Our Parts: Discovering Your True Self Through Internal Family Systems Therapy. Sounds True

Scott, J. G. (1928). "Trial Methods of the Inquisition." The Denver Bar Association Record V(8-9), Art. 2, Aug-Sept. pp. 3-10. https://digitalcommons.du.edu/cgi/viewcontent.cgi?article=6997&context=dlr

Scott, Ridley (2023). "The Life of J. Paul Getty, "the richest man in the history of the world"" Gentleman's Journal, April 1. https://www.thegentlemansjournal.com/article/life-j-paul-getty-richest-man-history-world

Singer, Emily, "How Dinosaurs Shrank and Became Birds," Quanta Magazine, https://www.quantamagazine.org/how-birds-evolved-from-dinosaurs-20150602/

Bibliography

Sun-Jin, Fo, Woo Yim, Hyeon, Bang, Myeong He, Lee, Mi ol, Jun, Tae-Youn, Choi, Jin-Sook, Lee, Myung-Soo, Lee, Won-Chul and Park, Yong-Moon (2011). "The Association between Economic Status and Depressive Symptoms: An Individual and Community Level Approach," Psychiatry Investigation, Aug 11.
https://www.ncbi.nlm.nih.gov/pmc/articles/PMC3182383/

The Gospel of Thomas, The Storytellers, https://www.pbs.org/wgbh/pages/frontline/shows/religion/story/thomas.html

"The Twelve Universal Laws," https://selfmadeladies.com/universal-laws/#universallaw6Thomason, Krista (2018). Naked: The Dark Side of Shame and Moral Life. Oxford University Press.

Tolle, E. (2001). The Power of Now: A Guide To Spiritual Enlightenment. New World Library.

UC Museum of Paleontology. "The Origin of Birds, Understanding Evolution." https://evolution.berkeley.edu/what-are-evograms/the-origin-of-birds/

The RNA World and the Origins of Life. National Library of Medicine, Molecular Biology of the Cell. 4th edition, https://www.ncbi.nlm.nih.gov/books/NBK26876/

Warner, Melanie, "Two Professors Found What Creates a Mass Shooter: Will Politicians Pay Attention?" Politico Magazine, 05/27/2022. https://www.politico.com/news/magazine/2022/05/27/stopping-mass-shooters-q-a-00035762

Watts, A. (1957). The Way of Zen. Pantheon Books.

Watts, A. (2000). What Is Zen. New World Library.

Weaver, I. (2020). "Epigenetics In Psychology." Noba. https://nobaproject.com/modules/epigenetics-in-psychology

Webb, Jonice, Ph.D., (2022). "Why Emotional Neglect Leaves People Feeling Flawed," Psychology Today. May 24.

Weingarden, Hilary, Reinshaw, Keith D., Wilhelm, Sabine, Tangney, June P. and DiMauro, Jennifer (2017). "Anxiety and Shame as Risk Factors for Depression, Suicidality, and Functional Impairment in Body Dysmorphic Disorder and Obsessive Compulsive Disorder," National Library of Medicine, PMC. Nov 1. https://www.ncbi.nlm.nih.gov/pmc/articles/PMC5026856/

Wikipedia, "Bacteriophage." https://en.wikipedia.org/wiki/Bacteriophage

Bibliography

Wikipedia, "Chögyam Trungpa." https://en.wikipedia.org/wiki/Ch%C3%B6gyam_Trungpa

Wikipedia, "Prokaryote." https://en.wikipedia.org/wiki/Prokaryote"

Willis, Henry A., Sosoo, Effua E., and Neblett, Enrique W. (2021). "The Associations Between Internalized Racism, Racial Identity, and Psychological Distress," Sage Journals, April 22. https://journals.sagepub.com/doi/full/10.1177/21676968211005598

Witvliet I, Margot, Kunst, Anton E., Onyebuchi, A Arah, Stronks, Karien (2013). "Sick regimes and sick people: A multilevel investigation of the population health consequences of perceived national corruption," Pub Med, October. https://pubmed.ncbi.nlm.nih.gov/24016030/

Bibliography

"Why We Think Perception Is Reality – Perception is a Reflection of You," Seeker Project 4 Spiritual Exploration (SP4SE), Techniques For Exploring Consciousness. https://seekerproject4se.org/2023/08/16/why-we-think-perception-is-reality-perception-is-a-reflection-of-you-an-individually-crafted-fiction/#:~:text=What%20we%20perceive%20is%20subject%20to%20various%20cognitive,is%20reality%2C%20and%20their%20reality%20cannot%20be%20questioned

Wolynn, M. "It Didn't Start with You: How inherited family trauma shapes who we are and how to end the cycle," https://www.youtube.com/watch?v=YqBhAgqZGSU

Zang, Yujie, (2022). "The Relationship Between Corruption Perception and Depression: A Multiple Mediation Model," Pub Med Aug. https://pubmed.ncbi.nlm.nih.gov/35935461/

Made in United States
Troutdale, OR
04/27/2025

30941042R00100